D1711400

A DICTIONARY OF TAXATION

A Dictionary of Taxation

Simon James

Reader in Economics, University of Exeter and Fellow of the Chartered Institute of Taxation, UK

Edward Elgar
Cheltenham, UK • Northampton, MA, USA

Published by
Edward Elgar Publishing Limited
8 Lansdown Place
Cheltenham
Glos GL50 2HU
UK

Edward Elgar Publishing, Inc.
6 Market Street
Northampton
Massachusetts 01060
USA

A catalogue record for this book
is available from the British Library

Library of Congress Cataloguing in Publication Data
James, Simon, 1952–
    A dictionary of taxation / Simon James.
        1. Taxation–Dictionaries.
    HJ2305.J328   1998
    336.2'003–dc21   97–35421
                                                       CIP

ISBN 1 85278 016 9 (cased)

Typeset by Manton Typesetters, 5-7 Eastfield Road, Louth, Lincolnshire LN11 7AJ, UK.
Printed and bound in Great Britain by Biddles Ltd, Guildford and King's Lynn

PREFACE

'In this world nothing can be said to be certain, except death and taxes'. It is not surprising that Benjamin Franklin's dictum[1] has been so widely quoted. Taxation of one sort or another can be traced back to the beginning of civilisation. Indeed it might be argued that taxes are the price of civilisation. Originally taxation was paid in kind – such as a share of the harvest, labour or objects of value. This was, of course, replaced by money as it became the basic means of exchange and increasingly in modern economies it is becoming possible to pay taxes electronically. Historically taxation has frequently been a driving force in administrative developments. For example in Ancient Rome the census was used to record the property of citizens for the purposes of taxation. The Domesday Book was a comprehensive record of ownership and liabilities of land in eleventh-century England and formed the basis of taxation for several centuries. Taxation is often the focus of struggles over resources. King John's demands for increased taxation brought on the crisis of 1215 which led to John's submission and the issue of the Magna Carta. It was a factor leading to the Civil War and the execution of Charles I and it was a major influence on the development of Parliament in the UK. Its role in the American revolution. 'No taxation without representation' is well known though one might agree with Callender:

> That a great reluctance to pay taxes existed in all the colonies, there can be no doubt. It was one of the marked characteristics of the American People long after their separation from England[2].

In modern economies taxation can absorb up to between a third and a half of national income. There is no significant part of a monetary economy which is unaffected by taxation, even if it is officially classified as 'tax-free'. One of the most obvious cases are 'duty-free' products at airports which are rarely priced so as to pass on the full benefit of their tax-free status to the final consumer. As basic economic analysis

---

1. Letter to Jean Baptiste Le Roy, 13 November 1789.
2. G.S. Callender, *Selections from the Economic History of the United States 1765–1860*, 1909, p. 23.

indicates, the effects of taxation work their way through the system by changes in prices, outputs, incomes and government expenditure.

The importance of taxation therefore seemed to make it a highly suitable subject for a dictionary of terms. It did not seem appropriate to set out to provide a complete collection of technical terms. That would have taken volumes even for a few tax systems and would not have been of major interest to many beyond those directly involved. Instead, the intention is to provide an explanation or description of terms which are commonly used or which provide interesting insights or curiosities of this most important of economic subjects.

In compiling a book of this sort I have incurred many debts. Edward Elgar has been a tremendously supportive and encouraging publisher and I hope he is pleased with the result. Many valuable contributions and comments have come from Roy Bartlett, Chris Evans, Abe Greenbaum, Robert Mitchell, Professor Christopher Nobes, Professor R.H. Parker, Ian Wallschutzky and many officials from the Australian Tax Office, the Inland Revenue, the Internal Revenue Service and Revenue Canada Taxation.

Simon James
University of Exeter

A

1040. The 'ten forty' or basic tax return used in the USA for personal income tax.

1040EZ. The 'ten forty e-zee' is the simplified version of the *1040* for US wage earners with little or no other income.

abatement. The cancellation of all or part of an assessed tax.

ability to earn. One way of viewing an individual's *ability to pay* tax. It has been suggested that it might form a good basis for taxation. However, while it is possible to measure what individuals actually earn, it is impossible to measure what they could earn.

ability to pay approach. Sometimes known as the *sacrifice approach*, this has a variety of manifestations but essentially holds that individuals should pay tax according to their means and not according to the benefits they receive from public expenditure. See also *benefit approach*.

absolute tax incidence. (1) The distributional effects of imposing a tax while holding the level of public expenditure constant. (2) The burden of a particular tax compared with a situation in which there are no taxes or public expenditure. See also *tax incidence, differential tax incidence* and *budget incidence.*

accelerated depreciation. Writing off the cost of fixed assets more quickly than on a straight line basis which, for example, would depreciate a £100 000 asset with a useful life of 10 years at £10 000 a year. Accelerated depreciation is often allowed for tax purposes, for example in the UK's system of *capital allowances.*

acceptable seal. A seal used to secure vehicles or storage areas for the purposes of revenue control.

accessions tax.   A cumulative tax imposed on the recipients of gifts and legacies. It provides a contrast to an *estate duty*, where tax liability is calculated on the basis of the value of the deceased's estate. Also known as an inheritance tax, or succession tax, it may be levied at progressive rates, and the relationship between the deceased and the recipient may be taken into account. It has been argued that accessions taxes have some advantages over taxes levied on the value of the estate. One advantage is based on an equity argument – that an accessions tax is based on the amounts received by the beneficiary rather than on the size of the estate. The other is that there may be a greater incentive to distribute wealth more evenly since the amount of tax will be lower for beneficiaries who have received less. A disadvantage is that the administrative costs of an accessions tax are likely to be significantly greater than for an estate duty.

FURTHER READING
Sandford, C.T., J.R.M. Willis and D.J. Ironside (1973), *An Accessions Tax*, London: Institute for Fiscal Studies.

accountant.   A general term describing someone who prepares and communicates financial and economic information but the term is normally taken to mean a professionally qualified accountant.

accounting period.   The period, usually a year, for which a person or business draws up accounts.

accounting standards.   Rules applied to the preparation of published financial statements and accounts and concerned with the quality of information available to investors and other users of financial information. As pointed out by Whittington, there is a natural tension between the requirements of financial reporting and the needs of a good tax base and this would appear to require a degree of separate development of accounting standards and tax rules.

FURTHER READING
McMahon, F. and P. Weetman (1997), 'Commercial accounting principles: questions of fact and questions of tax law', *British Tax Review*, 6–18.
Whittington, G. (1995) 'Tax policy and accounting standards', *British Tax Review*, 452–456.

accretion.   The value of a bond bought at a discount as it moves towards its face value at maturity. In the USA the Internal Revenue Service has specific provisions relating to such adjustments in value.

accruals basis. The principle that income (taxable or otherwise) should be measured on the basis of when transactions occur or values change rather than when cash is actually paid or received. For example, for capital gains tax the principle would involve valuing assets each year rather than when any capital gains or losses were actually realised.

accumulated earnings tax. US tax on accumulated taxable income of a corporation.

acqua vitae. From the Latin, meaning water of life, the term was used for the purposes of taxation to describe plain alcoholic spirit.

ACT. *Advance corporation tax.*

active fiscal policy. The active use of discretionary elements of *fiscal policy.*

active income. Income earned from current work effort and sometimes described as 'earned income'. It is contrasted with *unearned income, passive income* or *investment income.*

active trust. A *trust* in which the trustee has more obligations than simply handing over trust property when requested by a person entitled to it. See also *bare trust.*

actual incidence. The distribution of the burden of a tax in terms of reduced real incomes. The actual incidence may well be different from the *formal incidence* of the tax.

additional personal allowance. An extra *personal allowance* which increases the single allowance up to the value of the *married allowance.* It is mainly for single taxpayers with children.

adjudicator. The new post of Revenue Adjudicator was set up by the Inland Revenue in 1993. The role of the adjudicator is to consider complaints about the way in which the tax office has handled a person's tax affairs when the taxpayer is not satisfied with the Revenue's response. The role does not cover disputes concerning areas covered by existing rights of appeal, for example with respect to the interpretation of tax law or the amount of tax charged. Nor does it affect a taxpayer's right to approach the *Ombudsman* through a Member of Parliament.

administrative costs. The costs to the public sector of operating a tax or tax system. It is sometimes compared with the *compliance costs* imposed on the private sector.

FURTHER READING
Sandford, C.T., M. Godwin and P. Hardwick (1989), *Administrative and Compliance Costs of Taxation*, Bath: Fiscal Publications.

administrative lag. Also known as the *implementation lag*, it refers to the delay between a decision to alter fiscal policy and its implementation.

administrative review. A review made by an administrative rather than a judicial body. See also *judicial review*.

ad valorem **taxes.** Taxes based on the price or value of a good or service.

advance corporation tax. An early payment of *corporation tax* in the UK which is required when a company pays dividends to its shareholders. Advance corporation tax paid can be credited against *corporation tax liability* when that falls due, the remaining payment being described as *Mainstream Corporation tax*. One of the main purposes of advance corporation tax is that it is related to the tax credits issued with dividends under the *imputation system*. Such tax credits represent the advance corporation tax paid and can be set against taxpayers' liability to income tax. Advance corporation tax ensures that the tax credits represent corporation tax actually paid.

advance pricing agreements. Used by the Internal Revenue Service in the USA to determine appropriate prices in advance in *transfer pricing* situations.

advance ruling. A decision issued for the guidance of taxpayers on the tax consequences of a future possible transaction.

adventure in the nature of trade. UK legal term to describe trade which may be taxable. Under this concept a single transaction might be viewed as an adventure in the nature of trade and the profits subject to tax.

age allowance. A *personal allowance* granted to elderly people with modest incomes.

agent. A person who acts for another. Tax agents deal with their clients' tax affairs for a fee – also known as tax accountants or *tax practitioners*.

aggregation basis of taxation. The arrangement by which the incomes of members of a family are aggregated for the purpose of taxation. The usual contrast is with the *individual basis of taxation*. In the UK, when income tax was first introduced in 1799, a married man was responsible for declaring and accounting for his wife's income. In 1806 this arrangement was taken one stage further in that the 'profits' of a married woman were then deemed to be the 'profits' of her husband. This relic remained right up to 1990 when the law still stated that 'A woman's income chargeable to income tax shall ... [for any year] during which she is a married woman living with her husband be deemed for income tax purposes to be his income and not to be her income.' This arrangement was finally ended when the system of independent taxation was introduced in April 1990. See also *income splitting*.

agricultural levy. A levy made in accordance with the European Common Agricultural policy in respect of certain imported goods.

air passenger duty. A tax on passenger flights commencing in the UK. There is an exemption in respect of pleasure flights of less than an hour which begin and end at the same airport.

alcohol taxation. Alcohol is a prime target for taxation in some countries on account of its alleged harmful effects and price inelasticity. The subject of taxation is usually ethyl alcohol. Alcohol to be used for commercial purposes without incurring duty is mixed with methyl to make it unfit for drinking. Methylated spirits might contain about 10 per cent of pyroxylic spirit.

FURTHER READING
Cook, P.J. and M.J. Moor (1994), 'This tax's for you: The case for higher beer taxes', *National Tax Journal*, **XLVII**(3), 559–573.
Irvine, I.J. and W.A. Sims (1993), 'The welfare effects of alcohol taxation', *Journal of Public Economics*, **52**(1), 83–100.

alimony. Payments made by a spouse or former spouse as part of the arrangements of separation or divorce. In the UK such payments are more usually referred to as maintenance. Under some income tax regimes such payments, if compulsory, may be granted tax relief.

allocative function. One of the economic roles of government. The allocative function involves tax and expenditure relating to specific goods and services which it is thought might not be provided in appropriate quantities if markets were left to function independently. See also *distribution function* and *stabilisation function*.

allowances. The amounts of income a person can receive before being subject to income tax.

alternative minimum tax. A provision in some tax systems which requires taxpayers with substantial income to pay some minimum level of tax, even if they would not otherwise be subject to tax.

amnesty. In the case of tax, the opportunity to disclose to the authorities previously unpaid tax liability without attracting penalties.

FURTHER READING
Alm, J. and W. Beck (1993), 'Tax amnesties and compliance in the long run: A time series analysis', *National Tax Journal*, **XLVI**(1), 53–60.
Cassone, A. and C. Marchese (1995), 'Tax amnesties as special sales offers: the Italian experience', *Public Finance*, **50**(1), 51–66.
Crane, S.E. and F. Nourzad (1990), 'Tax rates and tax evasion: evidence from California amnesty data', *National Tax Journal*, **XLIII**(2), 189–199.

amortisation. Accounting method of spreading the cost of an asset over its useful life; usually applied to intangible assets. See also *depreciation*.

announcement effect. Changes in individuals' behaviour caused by the announcement of a tax. More precisely, it describes any differences in behaviour where a change in income is caused by a tax or by some other factor.

annual exemption. An amount which is free of tax in any one year – for example for the purposes of capital gains tax or inheritance tax.

annual return. A document completed by companies listing certain particulars and financial information and, in the UK, forwarded to the Registrar of Companies.

annuity. An investment which entitles the holder to a series of annual payments. The taxation of annuities can be more complex than some other investments because each of these payments might be considered to be partly interest and partly a repayment of the original capital sum invested. Where an annuity is paid tax-free at the *basic rate of tax* it is necessary to calculate the gross equivalent in order to determine any higher rate liability. If the payments are intended to be permanent, the investment is known as a perpetuity. The present value (*pv*) of a perpetuity is the sum paid in each period (*p*) divided by the discount rate (*r*). Hence:

$$pv = \frac{p}{r}$$

For example, a perpetuity which paid £100 a year when interest rates generally were, say, 10 per cent would be worth £1000:

$$\frac{100}{0.10} = £1000$$

anti-avoidance legislation. There is no general legal provision in the UK that transactions which reduce tax liability are void. The principle derived from the *Duke of Westminster* case indicated that courts should not look behind the legal *form* of a transaction to examine its substance. If the form was satisfactory then the transaction should have been allowed even if it were an entirely artificial event created only for the purpose of tax avoidance. However later decisions have taken more account of the substance of the transaction. See also *fraus legis doctrine* and *Ramsey principle*.

FURTHER READING
Maters, C. (1994), 'Is there a need for general anti-avoidance legislation in the United Kingdom?', *British Tax Review*, 647–673.

anti-dumping duty.   A levy imposed by a country on imports which it considers to be priced below the cost of production or unfairly subsidised in the exporting country.

anonymous letters.   As those who have worked in tax offices are aware, it is not unknown for the revenue authorities to receive letters alleging tax irregularities. Signed by a 'well wisher', 'honest taxpayer' or from an aggrieved spouse, neighbour, employee or business partner, the information is not always accurate but can lead to an investigation. Someone boasting about large amounts of tax evasion can lead another taxpayer sharing the good news with the tax office. You have been warned.

appeal.   A request for a decision to be changed. In the UK most appeals are settled between the taxpayer and the inspector. If no agreement can be reached, the appeal will be heard by the *Commissioners of Inland Revenue*. In his *Devil's Dictionary*, Ambrose Bierce defined an appeal as putting 'the dice into the box for another throw'.

FURTHER READING
Avery Jones, J.F. (1994), 'Tax appeals: the case for reform', *British Tax Review*, 3–18.

appreciation.   The increase in the value of an *asset*. The increase might only be a nominal one that is caused by an increase in prices generally and some tax systems make adjustments for inflation. A real increase in value occurs when the price of an asset increases relative to other prices.

arbitrage.   See *tax arbitrage*.

arm's length.   The concept describing transactions between parties dealing with each other independently.

artificial schemes.   Transactions set up only with the intention of avoiding tax. See *avoidance*.

art of taxation.   See *Colbert*.

ash cash.   Colloquial term for the fee payable to doctors for signing crematorium records. Medical practitioners have been known to omit such items from their accounts and it has led to further revenue investigations.

assessed taxes. An old form of taxation applying to taxable articles owned by individuals.

assessed valuation. The value put on an asset for tax purposes.

assessment. The process of calculating tax liability.

asset. Something of value controlled by an individual or a company. Tangible assets such as factories and machinery may be distinguished from intangible assets such as *goodwill*. A distinction is also made between 'real' assets such as machinery and financial assets such as stocks and shares.

assigned taxes. Taxes which are used to raise money for specific purposes rather than as a source of government expenditure generally. The more current term is *earmarking* taxes.

ATII. Associate of the Taxation Institute Incorporated. See *Chartered Institute of Taxation*.

attenuation charge. Excise charge related to the alcohol capable of being produced by the attenuation of the wort during fermentation.

audit. A tax audit is an investigation into the degree of truth and fairness of a taxpayer's books or accounts. A 'desk audit' refers to one undertaken at the tax office, a 'field audit' to one carried out at the taxpayer's premises or elsewhere outside the tax office.

FURTHER READING
Dubin, J.A., M.J. Graetz and L.L. Wilde (1990), 'The effect of audit rates on the federal individual income tax, 1977–1986', *National Tax Journal*, **XLIII**(4), 395–409.

audit trail. The chain of evidence that links an item in the accounts with documentary evidence verifying the transaction.

aulnager. In medieval times, an officer appointed to measure and inspect cloth. The responsibilities of the position may also have included the taxation of imported cloth.

authorised methylator.   A person authorised to methylate alcoholic spirit – that is to render it unfit to drink and so able to be used for commercial purposes without the imposition of the excise duty on alcohol.

automatic stabilisers.   Those parts of the taxation and public expenditure system which reduce fluctuations in the economy without the need for direct government action. For example, a progressive tax system would result in tax receipts changing proportionately more than any original change in national income. This would tend to cushion any decline in national income and dampen any increase. As the response is automatic, the *recognition lag* and at least part of the *implementation lag* are avoided. However, automatic stabilisers have certain limitations in that they cannot cope with large exogenous changes, they cannot eliminate economic cycles only dampen them and while they may alleviate economic depression they may also impede recovery. Automatic stabilisers are sometimes described as 'built-in flexibility'.

average rate of tax.   The amount of tax paid as a proportion of the tax base. The concept is primarily used with respect to income tax where it describes the proportion of a person's income paid in tax. It is therefore an indication of the effect a tax can have on a taxpayer's net income. In the analysis of the ways in which taxes can influence behaviour, this is known as the *income effect*. Taxpayers may also be influenced by the *marginal rate of tax* and the *substitution effect*.

averaging provisions.   Legislation permitting taxpayers to spread certain incomes over a number of years. The reason for such arrangements is that some incomes fluctuate considerably and, under a progressive tax system, will be taxed more heavily than if the same income were received in a steady stream.

avoidance.   Tax avoidance describes the rearrangement of a person's affairs, within the law, in order to reduce tax liability. In *Ayrshire Pullman Motor Services* v. *IRC* [1929] 14 TC 754 at p. 763, Lord Clyde gave as his opinion:

> No man in this country is under the smallest obligation, moral or other, so to arrange his legal relations to his business or to his property so as to enable the Inland Revenue to put the largest possible shovel into his stores.

The Inland Revenue is not slow – and quite rightly – to take every advantage which is open to it under the taxing statutes for the purpose of depleting the taxpayer's pocket. And the taxpayer is, in like manner, entitled to be astute to prevent, so far as he honestly can, the depletion of his means by the Revenue.

However the judicial view regarding tax avoidance has tightened somewhat. Lord Denning in *Re Weston's Settlements* [1969] 1 Ch. 223 at p. 245 stated 'The avoidance of tax may be lawful, but it is not yet a virtue'. The courts have made some further moves towards restricting its legality, for example see the *Ramsey principle*. Furthermore, in *Matrix Securities Ltd.* v. *IRC* [1994] STC 272 at p. 282, Lord Templeman said 'Every tax avoidance scheme involves a trick and a pretence. It is the task of the Revenue to unravel the trick and the duty of the court to ignore the pretence'. Nevertheless tax avoidance in general is considered a legitimate activity and is often contrasted with illegal tax *evasion*.

avoir fiscal. A tax credit accompanying the payment of dividends by French companies.

avoision. The term 'tax avoision' describes behaviour designed to reduce tax payments in areas where the law is unclear. It was coined to indicate that there is not always a clear distinction between tax *avoidance* and tax *evasion*.

FURTHER READING
Seldon, A. (ed.) (1979), *Tax Avoision: The Economic, Legal and Moral Inter-relationships between Avoidance and Evasion*, London: Institute of Economic Affairs.

B

bachelor duty. A tax on unmarried men and sometimes unmarried women. It is another way of achieving a tax concession for married couples.

back duty. Tax that is assessed by the tax office where tax has not been paid because of some fault on the part of the taxpayer – whether neglect or fraud.

back taxes. Another name for *back duty*.

backward bending supply curve of labour. The hypothesis that, as wages rise, after some point workers take part of their extra income in the form of additional leisure and work less. Therefore tax reductions might also encourage some people to work less. In Figure B.1 the graph shows the relationship between after-tax wage rate on the vertical axis and hours of work shown on the horizontal axis. As the after-tax wage rate rises, hours of work also rise until these reach a maximum at point M. As wages rise further hours of work fall. Thus, for example, a person with an after-tax wage of W_1 would wish to work H_1 hours of work. If a reduction in tax caused the after-tax wage to increase to W_2 the individual might choose to enjoy their higher level of income at least partly by reducing hours of work to H_2. See also *labour supply*.

FURTHER READING
James, S. and C. Nobes (1996), *The Economics of Taxation*, 5th edn., London: Prentice Hall.

bad debt. An account or loan which it is not possible to collect and is therefore written off.

bad debt relief. Tax relief in respect of *bad debts*.

balanced budget. A government budget where revenue equals expenditure.

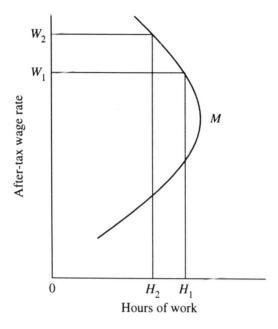

Figure B.1 A backward bending supply curve of labour

balanced budget multiplier. A measure of the final change in national income when government revenue and expenditure are increased by an equal amount. For example, if government spending and taxation were each increased by £1 billion and national income rose by £1 billion as a result, the balanced budget multiplier would be 1.

bankrupt. An insolvent person or organisation where the assets (if any) are administered by a court of law for the benefit of creditors. See also *tax bankruptcies*.

bare trust. A *trust* in which there is no obligation on the trustee except to transfer trust property when requested by a person entitled to it. There may be tax implications. For example, with a bare trust all capital gains and losses are normally those of the beneficiary and not the trustee. See also *active trust*.

basic income scheme.   A proposal that would replace the social security system, at least partly, with a general basic income for individuals. It is sometimes combined with a proposal for a *flat tax.*

FURTHER READING
Atkinson, A.B. (1995), *Public Economics in Action: The Basic Income/Flat Tax Proposal,* Oxford: Oxford University Press.

basic rate of tax.   The main rate of income tax. Tax may also be imposed at one or more higher rates on higher incomes and there may be a reduced rate on lower incomes.

basic relief.   Tax relief which is available to all regardless of their personal circumstances.

bearer levy.   A tax which is withheld from interest or dividends on bearer securities. Bearer securities are stocks or shares which are traded without registering the change of ownership. The person who owns the certificate has the right to the income from the security, which is usually received using coupons. Since the owner of bearer securities is anonymous, there may be a temptation to conceal the income from the tax authorities. Many countries therefore either ban bearer securities altogether or impose a high bearer levy.

bed and breakfast.   Selling securities and repurchasing them within 24 hours in order to establish a capital gain or loss.

beneficial loan arrangement.   A loan in which interest is below market rates and which, in certain circumstances, is chargeable to tax.

beneficial occupation.   The occupation of property at less than the market rent. Such a benefit may be brought into tax.

beneficial owner.   The person who benefits from an asset. This might be different from the legal owner, who may be a nominee.

benefit approach.   The benefit principle of taxation holds that the amount of tax each individual pays should be determined by the amount of benefit he or she receives from public expenditure. The implication is that government revenue and expenditure should not alter the distribution of income. There are several difficulties with this approach, not the least of which is that it is very difficult to measure the impact of public expenditure on everyone's incomes. See also *ability to pay approach.*

benefits in kind.   Income which is paid in some form other than cash. Examples include a company car, cheap accommodation or free meals. Benefits in kind are often required to be included as part of a person's *taxable income.*

FURTHER READING
Horsman, E.G. (1995), 'The taxation of benefits in kind: A way out of the muddle?', Parts I and II, *British Tax Review*, 150–155 and 317–324.

benefit tax.   A tax related to the benefit received from a government service. See *benefit approach.*

Benford's Law.   Is based on expected frequencies in the form of tabulated data and has been suggested as a way to detect tax and other fraud. It might be expected that, for any natural number, there is not an 11.11% chance of each digit appearing first (that is, that digits 1 to 9 do not have an equal chance of appearing first in any number). However it is also untrue that second and subsequent digits have an equal chance of appearing. Frank Benford tabulated the frequencies of a variety of geographical and scientific data and using mathematical arguments derived the expected frequencies of combination shown in Table B.1. For example, according to Benford's Law, the chance of zero being the second digit in any number is not 0.1 but 0.12.

Researchers have found that reported net income of corporations have more second digit 0s and less second digit 9s than expected. This might indicate, therefore, that those producing the accounts might think that, say, 10 001 725 looks significantly more than 9 976 391 and that such an upward manipulation would be worthwhile. Benford's Law also has an immediate application in identifying possible under-reporting of income in tax returns. Nigrini (1992) has measured an apparent distortion for 200 000 US individual income tax returns.

FURTHER READING
Benford, F. (1938), 'The law of anomalous numbers', *Proceedings of the American Philosophical Society*, **78**, 551–572.
Nigrini, M.J. (1992), *The Detection of Income Tax Evasion Through an Analysis of Digital Distributions*, PhD Dissertation, Department of Accounting, University of Cincinnati.

Table B.1 Benford's Law: Expected digital frequencies

Digit	1st	2nd	3rd	4th
0		.11968	.10178	.10018
1	.30103	.11389	.10138	.10014
2	.17609	.10082	.10097	.10010
3	.12494	.10433	.10057	.10006
4	.09691	.10031	.10018	.10002
5	.07918	.09668	.09979	.09998
6	.06695	.09337	.09940	.09994
7	.05799	.09035	.09902	.09990
8	.05115	.08757	.09864	.09986
9	.04576	.08500	.09827	.09982

Nigrini, M.J. (1993), 'Can Benford's Law be used in forensic accounting?', *The Balance Sheet*, June.

bereavement allowance. A tax allowance granted to an individual following the death of a spouse.

betterment levy. A tax on the increase in the value of real property. One of the justifications for such a tax is that the value of property is partly determined by the local infrastructure and other factors which are not provided by the owner. It has therefore been thought that some of the increase in property values generated in this way should be returned to society through taxation.

betting duty. A tax on betting made with a bookmaker.

bingo duty. A levy imposed on bingo played on licensed premises.

black economy. Economic activity which is not declared for tax purposes and, more generally, illegal economic activity. Also known as the *moonlight economy* or the underground economy.

blob analysis. Tables of comparative tax systems where a range of taxes are listed and their presence in any particular country is indicated with a blob. For example, income tax is invariably included in the list, and any country which has such a tax gets a blob under income tax. One limitation of such an approach is that taxes might have the same name but be very different taxes. See also *classification of taxes*.

blue return system.   A system introduced in Japan by the *Shoup Mission* and intended to improve taxpayers' accounting systems and to encourage honest self-assessment. Taxpayers who maintain the proper accounts required by the blue return system and report their income correctly are given certain privileges.

FURTHER READING
An Outline of Japanese Taxes (1993), Tokyo: Printing Bureau, Ministry of Finance.

Board of Inland Revenue.   See *Inland Revenue*.

Board of Stamps.   Constituted in 1694 to administer *stamp duties*.

Board of Taxes.   Established in 1784 to manage the 'assessed taxes' levied on luxuries such as carriages and racehorses. It was amalgamated with the Board of Stamps in 1833 to become the Board of Stamps and Taxes and with the Board of Excise in 1849 to become the Board of *Inland Revenue*. The administration of excise duties was transferred to *Customs & Excise* in 1909.

bodies of persons.   Collective term used for the purposes of taxation. Except where the circumstances are inappropriate, bodies of persons means any body politic, corporate or collegiate, and any company, fraternity and society of persons whether corporate or not corporate. – T.A. 1988, s. 832 (1).

FURTHER READING
Avery Jones, J.F. (1991), 'Bodies of persons', *British Tax Review*, 453–465.

bond.   A financial guarantee to secure the payment of duty.

bonded warehouse.   A secure warehouse where taxable goods may be stored without payment of tax. Frequently there are two locks, the key to one being kept by the tax department. The owner of the warehouse or the trader may be required to put up a *bond* to cover any tax loss in case the goods are removed without tax being paid.

bond washing. The practice of turning taxable income into capital by selling a security 'cum interest' or 'cum dividend' and repurchasing it 'ex interest' or 'ex dividend'. The income from the security is then payable to someone else and this should be reflected in a lower repurchase price. If capital gains are taxed less heavily than income there may be some tax advantage in this practice, but under many tax regimes such advantages are restricted or prevented altogether.

Boston tea party. One of the events in the process of American Independence which took place when the then colonists rejected British taxes on tea.

FURTHER READING
Labaree, B.W. (1964), *The Boston Tea Party*, Oxford: Oxford University Press.

bottom of the harbour schemes. These schemes obstructed the collection of tax by arranging for the tax to be payable by a company or trustee which was stripped of all its assets. The expression comes from the assumption that the relevant books and documents disappeared – possibly to the bottom of the harbour. These schemes took root in Australia in the 1970s but are now largely obsolete as a result of legislation.

bracket creep. The process by which inflation pushes taxpayers into higher tax bands if the different tax brackets are not indexed to price changes. See also *fiscal drag*.

brackets. The ranges of *taxable income*, wealth and so on which are subject to different rates of tax. For example, an income tax might be imposed at 20 per cent on the first £5000 of taxable income, 25 per cent on the next £5000, 30 per cent on the next £10 000 and so on. These bands of taxable income may be referred to as the 25 per cent tax bracket and so on.

broad based taxes. Taxes imposed on a wide range of goods and services. Such taxes are thought less likely to distort economic choices by imposing an *excess burden* on an economy than more narrowly based taxes might.

Brookings Institution. An independent US research centre which produces influential research reports on subjects including taxation.

Budget. The Budget is the occasion on which the Chancellor of the Exchequer introduces the proposed changes to taxation. Since 1993, it has normally been presented in November each year. Budget day can be something of a fiscal event with frequent surprises, and it has developed over many years. One of the most notable Budgets was Gladstone's of 1853. This was his first of 13 budgets – his last was in 1882. It was a record breaker. The Budget speech lasted five hours and is recorded by over 72 columns of Hansard. In many ways it laid the basis of the Budget ritual as we know it today. The famous red box dates from this time and Gladstone took the office of Chancellor of the Exchequer from a relatively humble role to one of major significance. Although the Financial Statement shown in Table B.2 looks simple compared to modern versions, the 1853 Budget already featured some of the complexity of its twentieth-century successors.

Table B.2   Summary of the Financial Statement of the Chancellor of the Exchequer, 1853

Estimated Revenue		Estimated Expenditure	
Customs	20,680,000	Funded debt	27,500,000
Excise	14,640,000	Unfunded debt	304,000
Stamps	6,700,000		27,804,000
Taxes	3,250,000	Consolidated Fund	2,503,000
Income tax	5,550,000	Army	6,025,000
Post Office	900,000	Navy	6,235,000
Crown Lands	390,000	Ordnance	3,053,000
Miscellaneous	320,000	Civil Estimates	4,476,000
Old Stores	460,000	Commissariat	557,000
Anticipated Saving from Reduction of		Militia	530,000
the 3 per cents	100,000	Caffre War	200,000
		Packet Service	800,000
	52,990,000		52,183,000

Estimated surplus, £807,000

Source: Hansard, 18 April 1853, cols. 1423–4.

budgetary policy. Strategy with respect to the government's revenue and expenditure. See *fiscal policy*.

budget incidence. The final effect of government spending and taxation on a household. See *incidence of taxation*.

budget year. The 12-month fiscal *year*.

built-in flexibility. See *automatic stabilisers*.

buoyancy. The extent to which the revenues of a particular tax are maintained or increased with inflation or with increases in real per capita income. Taxes linked to prices, such as VAT, will keep up with inflation. Income taxes which are progressive will raise increasing revenue and are therefore even more buoyant. The revenue from specific taxes which are linked to the quantities of goods and services, rather than their prices, will fall behind in real terms unless the taxes are increased in line with inflation. Local authority *rates* provided another example as their revenue did not appear to keep pace with inflation and local public spending requirements.

burden. See *tax burden*.

burnout. US term for taxpayers drawing taxable profits from their investments after all available tax relief has been exploited.

Business economic notes. Notes produced by the Inland Revenue to guide inspectors in their evaluation of the accuracy of accounts in different businesses.

business entertainment expenses. A form of expenditure which only attracts tax relief in certain restricted circumstances, for example if it is for *overseas customers*.

business rates. A tax levied on non-domestic property in the UK. See also *rates*.

FURTHER READING
Bond, S., K. Denny, J. Hall and W. McClusky, (1996), 'Who pays business rates?', *Fiscal Studies*, **17** (1), 19–35.

C

canons of taxation.   *Adam Smith's* famous four canons of taxation are:

I. The subjects of every state ought to contribute towards the support of the government, as nearly as possible in proportion to their respective abilities; this is, in proportion to the revenue which they respectively enjoy under the protection of the state ... .

II. The tax which each individual is bound to pay, ought to be certain, and not arbitrary. The time of payment, the manner of payment, ought to be clear and plain to the contributor, and to every other person ... .

III. Every tax ought to be levied at the time, or in the manner in which it is most likely to be convenient for the contributor to pay it ... .

IV. Every tax ought to be so contrived as both to take out and to keep out of the pockets of the people as little as possible over and above what it brings into the public treasury of state.

FURTHER READING
Smith, A. (1776), *Wealth of Nations*, bk V, ch. II, pt. II, 'Of Taxes'.

capital allowances.   The UK system for providing for depreciation of assets with respect to taxation. Capital allowances are available for expenditure on *plant and machinery*, commercial buildings located in an *enterprise zone*, agricultural and industrial buildings, and hotels. Different categories of expenditure are treated differently. One of the main categories covers plant and machinery which attract a 25 per cent writing-down allowance. This is calculated on the balance of the 'pool' of expenditure at the end of the year. For example, suppose a trader had already spent £80 000 on plant and machinery and received £20 000 in capital allowances. In the tax year in question the trader purchases a further £40 000 on machinery. The pool in that tax year would be as follows:

	£
Written-down value brought forward	60 000
Add expenditure during the year	40 000
	100 000
Less writing-down allowance at 25%	25 000
Written-down value carried forward	75 000

FURTHER READING
Bond, S , K. Denny and M. Devereux (1993), 'Capital allowances and the impact of corporation tax on investment in the UK', *Fiscal Studies* **14** (2), 1–14.

capital appreciation bond.   A bond which pays no interest but investors gain by buying the bond at a discount and receiving the face value on maturity.

capital consumption. *Depreciation.*

capital export neutrality.   An arrangement whereby the same tax rate applies whether an investment is made in another country or in the domestic economy.

capital gains tax.   A tax on the increase in the value of assets. In the UK a tax on short-term gains was introduced in 1962 and a more comprehensive tax from 1965. One of the main arguments for the tax is that capital gains are really a form of income and should be taxed in a similar way. This was explained by the Chancellor of the Exchequer in his 1988 Budget speech as follows:

> In principle, there is little economic difference between income and capital gains, and many people effectively have the option of choosing to a significant extent which to receive. And in so far as there is a difference, it is by no means clear why one should be taxed more heavily than the other. Taxing them at different rates distorts investment decisions and inevitably creates a major tax avoidance industry.

FURTHER READING
Auerbach, A.J. (1989), 'Capital gains taxation and tax reform', *National Tax Journal,* **XLII** (3), 391–401.

capital goods.   Items purchased as part of the fixed capital of a business, rather than for processing, resale or consumption. It follows that sales taxes and so on treat capital goods differently from other goods.

capital income tax.   A tax on investment income.

capitalisation.   The effect on the price of an asset when a tax affects the yield of that asset. This happens because the capital value of an asset reflects the income (pecuniary and non-pecuniary) the asset is expected to yield. It follows that, if a tax changes the expected yield of an asset, it will also change its market price.

FURTHER READING
Do, A.Q. and C.F. Sirmans (1994), 'Residential property tax capitalisation: Discount rate evidence from California', *National Tax Journal*, **XLVII** (2), 341–348.

capitalisation of profits. The process whereby the profits of a company are converted into capital rather than being paid out as dividends. This can be done, for example, by issuing shareholders with bonus shares.

capital tax. A tax on the value of assets.

capital transfer tax. A cumulative tax on the transfer of wealth during life or on death. One of the intentions of the tax, in the words of the then Chancellor of the Exchequer, Denis Healey, was to form part of 'a determined attack on the maldistribution of wealth in Britain'. Although capital transfer tax was a major extension of the *estate duty* it replaced in 1975, it never raised as much revenue, as a percentage of gross domestic product, as estate duty had. Furthermore its scope was soon reduced and significant concessions continued to be made throughout its existence. Finally in 1986 it was subject to some reform and renamed *inheritance tax*.

capitation tax. A tax on each person – see *poll tax*.

carbon taxes. Taxes on fossil fuels: for example, coal, gas and petrol. The purposes of such taxation include the protection of the environment and restraint on the consumption of non-renewable energy sources.

FURTHER READING
Cnossen, S. and H. Vollebergh (1992), 'Toward a global excise on carbon', *National Tax Journal*, **XLV** (1), 23–36.
Symons, E., J. Proops and P. Gay (1994), 'Carbon taxes, consumer demand and carbon dioxide emissions: A simulation analysis for the UK', *Fiscal Studies* **15** (2), 19–43.

carry over. A provision whereby losses in excess of those allowable in one tax year may be set against income or gains in later tax years.

car tax. A tax on the value of new cars in the UK. It was abolished in 1992.

Carter Commission. A Canadian Royal Commission on taxation. Its six-volume report published in 1966 generated a great deal of discussion. The basic philosophy of the Commission was that there should be a very wide concept of income and the adoption of a wider income tax base would allow considerable reductions in tax rates. It is a view which has been echoed many times.

FURTHER READING
Carter Commission (1966), *Report of the Royal Commission on Taxation*, Ottawa: Queen's Printer.

cascade taxes.   See *turnover tax*.

cash economy.   That part of the economy in which transactions are conducted in cash. This may be used for a number of purposes including *tax evasion*. See also *black economy*.

cash hoard stories.   Sometimes advanced by taxpayers as the source of otherwise unexplained money. This is unlikely to convince the revenue authorities particularly if the taxpayer had small amounts saved on deposit or had been borrowing for normal items of expenditure.

CATA.   The Commonwealth Association of Tax Administrators set up at the Commonwealth Finance Ministers' meeting in 1976.

census.   In ancient Rome the census was a register of the property of citizens for the purposes of taxation. The term has also been used to mean a tax or tribute, especially a *poll tax*. The word derives from the Latin *censere*, to assess.

Centre 1.   The first of what were to be a small number of large computer centres for the administration of *PAYE*. It is located in East Kilbride and deals with PAYE in Scotland. That particular arrangement was not followed in later developments where the policy shifted towards centralising the computers but not the tax offices.

certainty.   This is one of the requirements of a 'good' tax since it facilitates rational economic decision making. Taxpayers should be able to calculate with certainty the amount of tax they would be liable to pay in different circumstances.

CGT. *Capital gains tax.*

Chancellor of the Exchequer. The Finance Minister in the UK.

charities. A non-profit organisation run for the benefit of others, especially those in need. Charities may benefit from certain tax concessions and taxpayers may be able to reduce their tax liabilities by donating to them.

FURTHER READING
Auten, G.E., J.M. Cilke and W.C. Randolf (1992), 'The effects of tax reform on charitable contributions', *National Tax Journal*, **XLV** (3), 267–290.
Boatsman, J.R. and S. Gupta (1996), 'Taxes and corporate charity: empirical evidence from micro-level panel data', *National Tax Journal*, **XLIX** (2), 193–213.
Ghosh, I.J. and M.H. Robson (1993), 'Charity and consideration', *British Tax Review*, 496–503.

charter. A written document recognising rights and so on. See also *taxpayers' charter* and *Magna Carta.*

Chartered Institute of Taxation. The Institute of Taxation was formed in December 1930. Their coat of arms shows a shield with a chequerboard since in former times a chequered table cloth had been used to check computations and a wheatsheaf marked with a Roman X to signify the old *tithe.* The shield is supported by two owls to signify the wisdom of tax officials and tax practitioners respectively, standing on an even balance. The members are qualified to advise on tax matters. There are two classes of membership – associates and fellows denoted by ATII and FTII respectively (Associate, or Fellow, of the Taxation Institute Incorporated). In addition to being a professional body, the Institute promotes research and informed discussion on tax matters. The Institution gained its Royal Charter in 1994. Their address is 12 Upper Belgrave Street, London, SW1X 8BB.

Chartered tax adviser. Member of the Chartered Institute of Taxation.

chattels. A tangible, movable asset. Examples include items of furniture. See also *immovable property.*

child allowance. A *personal allowance* for dependent children. In the UK child tax allowances have been replaced by cash payments in the form of child benefit.

church tax. A levy made by an officially recognised religion on its members on the basis of legislation.

CIT. *Comprehensive income tax.*

classical system of taxation. A corporate system of taxation under which profits are subject to corporation tax and then distributed profits are subject to personal income tax in the hands of the shareholders. It had been thought that it was desirable to encourage companies to plough their profits back into the business and this could be achieved by the imposition of higher rates of tax on distributed profits. However, more sophisticated thinking suggests that it might be better not to discriminate against distributed profits. See *imputation system.*

classification of taxes. Taxes may be defined in many ways, for example between current taxes on the flow of something and capital taxes on the stock of something. The OECD Classification is given in Table C.1. See also *blob analysis* and *tax.*

Table C.1   The OECD classification of taxes

1000   Taxes on goods and services
    1100   Taxes on the production, sale, transfer, leasing and delivery of goods and rendering of services
        1110   General taxes
        1120   Taxes on specific goods and services
            1121   Excises
            1122   Fiscal monopolies
            1123   Customs and import duties
            1124   Taxes on exports
            1125   Taxes on specific services
            1126   Other taxes
    1200   Taxes in respect of ownership and use of, or permission to use, goods or to perform activities
        1210   Recurrent taxes
            1211   Paid by households in respect of motor vehicles
            1212   Paid by others in respect of motor vehicles

Table C.1   continued

         1213   Paid in respect of other goods
    1220   Other taxes

2000   Taxes on income, profits and capital gains
    2100   Paid by households and institutions
         2110   On income and profits
         2120   On capital gains
    2200   Paid by corporate enterprises
         2210   On income and profits
         2220   On capital gains

3000   Social security contributions
    3100   Paid by employees
    3200   Paid by employers
    3300   Paid by self-employed or non-employed persons

4000   Taxes on employers based on payroll or manpower

5000   Taxes on net wealth and immovable property
    5100   Recurrent taxes on net wealth
    5110   Paid by households
    5120   Paid by corporate enterprises
    5200   Recurrent taxes on immovable property
    5210   Paid by households
    5220   Paid by enterprises
    5230   Paid by institutions and so on
    5300   Non-recurrent taxes on net wealth and immovable property
    5310   On net wealth
    5320   On immovable property

6000   Taxes and stamp duties on gifts, inheritances and on capital and financial transactions
    6100   On gifts and inheritances
         6110   Gifts
         6120   Inheritances
    6200   On capital and financial transactions

7000   Other taxes
    7100   Paid solely by enterprises
    7200   Other

claw back. A charge to tax which arises in retrospect through some change in anticipated circumstances. The term has also been used where an allowance has been specifically paid for by additional taxation.

close company. A company controlled by a small number of people. In the UK it is a company controlled by its directors or five or fewer persons or families. For the purposes of taxation, close companies fall between individuals operating as sole traders and partners paying income tax and corporations paying tax without reference to their owners' tax circumstances.

FURTHER READING
Plesko, G.A. (1995), '"Gimme shelter" – closely held corporations since tax reform', *National Tax Journal*, **XLVIII** (3), 409–416.

code. A device used within the UK cumulative *PAYE* scheme to represent allowances and deductions due to a taxpayer in order to determine the amount of income tax withheld. See also *tax code*.

Colbert, Jean Baptiste (1619–1683). Finance Minister to Louis XIV. He is attributed with the saying: 'The art of taxation consists in so plucking the goose as to obtain the largest possible amount of feathers with the smallest amount of hissing'.

collectors of taxes. Officials with the responsibility of collecting taxes, as opposed to assessing them, which has been the traditional responsibility of *inspectors of taxes*. The separation of the assessment and collection functions of income tax is logical in that those involved in assessment have no interest in the process of collection and vice versa. At one time it was even thought that the maintenance of security was so important that inspectors of taxes were forbidden to lodge in the same house as a collector.

FURTHER READING
Johnston, Sir Alexander (1965), *The Inland Revenue*, London: Allen and Unwin.

Commissioners of Income Tax. Individuals appointed to hear tax appeals concerning taxation in the UK. There are two categories of Commissioners – the General Commissioners who are unpaid members of the public and Special Commissioners who are lawyers with extensive experience of tax law. It has been said that if a taxpayer's case is 'an appeal to the heart' it is better if it were heard by the General Commissioners and by the Special Commissioners if there is a good legal argument.

FURTHER READING
Colley, R. (1996), 'General commissioners of income tax: Reasons for decisions', *British Tax Review*, 3, 312–318.
Sabine, B. (1992), 'Procedural rules for general and special commissioners', *British Tax Review*, 82–87.
Stebbings, C. (1993), 'The general commissioners of income tax: Assessors or adjudicators?', *British Tax Review*, 52–64.

commodity tax. A tax on goods.

community charge. A form of *poll tax* introduced in Scotland in 1989 and England and Wales in 1990. To promote *perceptibility*, the tax was payable by all adults at a flat rate set by the local authority. Some financial assistance was available to individuals on very low incomes but everyone was required to make a minimum payment of 20 per cent of the tax. For the great majority of individuals it was unrelated to any concept of *ability to pay*. The UK faced a considerable anti-tax campaign which included civil disobedience and a major riot in London. It has been argued that it was a contributory factor in the downfall of Mrs Margaret Thatcher as Prime Minister and it was replaced with the *council tax* in 1993.

FURTHER READING
Gibson, J. (1990), *The Politics and Economics of the Poll Tax: Mrs Thatcher's Downfall*, Warley: EMAS.
Smith, P. (1991), 'Lessons from the British poll tax disaster', *National Tax Journal*, pt. 2, **XLIV** (4), 421–436.

commutation. A reduction in a punishment, including one imposed by revenue authorities for non-compliance.

compliance. The willingness of taxpayers to act in accordance with the statutory requirements or intentions of the tax law and administration. Sometimes the definition of compliance is cast in terms of the extent to which taxpayers comply with the tax law. It has then been said that the degree of non-compliance can be measured by the 'tax gap' – the difference between actual revenue and that which would be received if there were 100 per cent compliance. This is too simplistic for practical policy purposes since successful tax administration requires taxpayers to comply without the need for enquiries, reminders or the threat or application of sanctions. It also requires them to respond on time. Furthermore if taxpayers go to inordinate lengths to reduce their tax liability, this could hardly be considered 'compliance' even if their activities are technically lawful. A full definition should therefore include compliance with the spirit as well as the letter of the law.

FURTHER READING
James, S. and I. Wallschutzky (1995), 'The shape of future tax administration', *Bulletin for International Fiscal Documentation*, **49** (5), 204–212.
Slemrod, J. (ed.) (1992), *Why People Pay Taxes: Tax Compliance and Enforcement*, Ann Arbor: The University of Michigan Press.

compliance costs.   The costs to the private sector of complying with the requirements of a tax.

FURTHER READING
Sandford, C.T., M. Godwin and P. Hardwick (1989), *Administrative and Compliance Costs of Taxation*, Bath: Fiscal Publications.

composite rate tax.   A withholding tax imposed on bank and building society interest in the UK. It was abolished in 1991 but provides an interesting example of the triumph of administrative simplicity over equity considerations. The composite rate of tax was calculated by estimating the tax liability of all the recipients of the interest, including both taxpayers and non-taxpayers. This was to the advantage of the taxpayers, since tax was withheld at a lower rate than would otherwise have applied but non-taxpayers could not obtain a rebate.

comprehensibility.   In a tax context, the degree with which a tax system is capable of being understood by taxpayers. Unfortunately it is too often something less than comprehensible. See also *fiscal fog* and *simplicity*.

FURTHER READING
James, S., A. Lewis and F. Allison (1987), *The Comprehensibility of Taxation*, Aldershot: Avebury.
Prebble, J. (1994), 'Why is tax law incomprehensible?', *British Tax Review*, 380–393

comprehensive income tax (CIT).   The essential idea is to tax the accretion of spending power and so, in its pure form, a comprehensive income tax base would include capital gains, windfalls and inheritances.

FURTHER READING
Meade, J.E. (1978), *The Structure and Reform of Direct Taxation*, London: IFS/Allen & Unwin, ch. 7.

conditional sale. A contract which cannot be enforced until a specific condition is satisfied. This might be relevant, for example, for capital gains tax. The date of the disposal of an asset would be the date the condition was satisfied rather than the date on which the contract was signed. If the condition were not satisfied then the sale need not proceed.

conduit company. A company through which earnings from foreign countries can be channelled to a holding company in a country with lower tax rates or in a *tax haven*.

congestion tax. A tax used to restrict the use of some facility at congested periods. One example is the idea of charging road users at peak times to ease congestion. The economic rationale is that usage will then be restricted to those who value the usage the most, or at least those who are able and willing to pay the congestion tax.

consolidated tax return. US term for the tax returns of a company and its US subsidiaries which are owned 80 per cent or more.

consolidation act. Legislation which repeals and re-enacts existing legislation concerned with a particular area.

FURTHER READING
Bramwell, R. (1992), 'Interpreting consolidation acts: The influence of history', *British Tax Review*, 69–75.

consumption tax. A tax on expenditures other than investment expenditure. See *expenditure tax*.

contingent considerations. The contractual agreement that a purchaser of an asset should pay additional sums should certain circumstances arise in the future. This can arise in respect of some purchases of shares or land. The treatment of contingent considerations for capital gains tax purposes can be complicated.

contingent liabilities. A sale may take place where the contract includes contingent liabilities in that it requires some of the proceeds to be returned in the future in certain circumstances. Normally any assessment to capital gains tax in this respect arises only if a contingent liability becomes an actual liability.

corporate income tax. A tax on companies. See *corporate taxation and corporation tax.*

corporate taxation. Taxes relating to incorporated enterprises. The UK version is *corporation tax*. Sometimes it is asked why companies should be taxed as well as individuals since ultimately corporations are wholly owned by individuals. The main reasons involve the comparative treatment of unincorporated and incorporated enterprises. Unincorporated businesses consist of sole traders and partnerships and their profits are subject to income tax each year at the appropriate rates. Incorporated enterprises have a legal existence separate from their owners. This allows profits to be retained within the business and so avoid income tax until such time as they are distributed as dividends.

The absence of a corporation tax would provide a considerable tax advantage for incorporated enterprises in respect of retained profits. This might be considered disadvantageous on grounds of both efficiency and equity. It might be inefficient because firms which are generating high profits now might not be the same as the firms with the best investment prospects for the future. It might be better, therefore, if there were no particular tax incentives to retain profits in the firms which generated them. When firms distribute profits, shareholders are then able to reinvest them where there are the best hopes for the future. Furthermore it may be inefficient to provide tax incentives to incorporate when there may be other reasons for preferring to remain unincorporated. On equity grounds, of course, it would be unfair to treat the incorporated and unincorporated businesses too differently.

A second argument put forward for a corporation tax is that tax revenue is needed and, given the costs of raising taxes, a tax on companies might be less inefficient or less undesirable in other ways than alternative sources of revenue.

A third argument relates to the benefit approach to taxation. This view is that incorporated enterprises have certain privileges, in particular that they are entities which are legally separate from their owners and that the shareholders have limited liability for the business's debts. However, there are problems with the benefit approach; it is difficult to measure the benefit of these privileges, and companies have certain legal obligations, as well as benefits.

A fourth point relates not to the benefits of introducing a new corporation tax, but to the effects of abolishing an existing one. It has been suggested that 'an old tax is a good tax' because everyone has adjusted to it. So, for instance, the prices of company shares are lower than they would be in the absence of a tax on company profits. If a corporation tax were abolished, the *capitalisation* effect would mean an increase in share prices. This would provide a windfall capital gain to existing shareholders but might do nothing to generate new investment in the corporate sector.

Another viewpoint is that taxing company profits is a way of putting extra tax on unearned, as opposed to earned income. However, even if it were considered desirable to discriminate against investment income, such a tax would not cover other forms of it, namely interest and rent. Finally it has been argued that a corporation tax might increase 'fiscal flexibility' in relation to the tax treatment of companies but this would not seem to be particularly convincing. See also *corporation tax*.

FURTHER READING
Cnossen, S. (1996), 'Company taxes in the European Union: Criteria and options for reform', *Fiscal Studies*, **17** (4), 67–97.
Gammie, M. (1992), 'Reforming corporate taxation: An evaluation of the United States Treasury integration proposals and other corporate tax systems in an international context', pts. I and II, *British Tax Review*, 148–173 and 243–276.
Mintz, J. (1995), 'The corporation tax: A survey', *Fiscal Studies*, **16** (4), 23–68.
Stitt, I.P.A. (1993), 'Corporate taxation in the EC', *British Tax Review*, 75–89.

corporation. An organisation with its own legal identity which is separate and distinct from its legal owners, the shareholders. See *incorporation*.

corporation tax. A tax on the 'chargeable profits' of a company, that is income and chargeable gains. Such taxes have been classified into three types – the *classical system*, the *imputation system* and the *split-rate system*. See also *corporate taxation*.

corrective tax. A tax used to offset an economic distortion in the economy. See, for example, *congestion tax* and *external effect*.

corvée. The requirement to give one's personal labour to the government. This appears to be one of the earliest form of taxation and requirements for individuals to work on public projects can be traced back to ancient times.

council tax. A local domestic property tax introduced in the UK in 1991 to replace the disastrous *community charge*. It is based on the value of property, which for this purpose is placed in different bands. It has retained a surviving element of the community charge or 'poll tax', in that there is a 25 per cent reduction for households containing a single adult.

FURTHER READING
Sparkes, P. (1992), 'Definitional issues of the English council tax legislation', *British Tax Review*, 305–322.

countervailing duty. A levy on imports designed to offset a subsidy paid by the exporting country.

crowding out. The effect that an increase in public expenditure might reduce private sector consumption or investment or both. This can happen, for instance, if the additional public expenditure puts pressure on the money supply and this causes an increase in interest rates. Crowding out is one of the possible limitations of *fiscal policy*.

crummy trust. US term for a trust fund which can be used to avoid federal gift taxes.

CTO. Capital Taxes Office.

cumulation. A method of withholding tax at source so that the amount of tax withheld in any one week or month is based on the cumulated total of taxable income (gross income less allowances) since the beginning of the tax year. It may be illustrated with an example. Suppose there is a single rate of tax of 25 per cent and a taxpayer is entitled to £4160 worth of allowances or 'free pay' which may be received before tax is levied. In Table C.2, the taxpayer's allowances are divided by the number of pay periods in the tax year – 52 weeks for this individual. The individual therefore has £80 worth of free pay each period which is cumulated as the tax year progresses (in column 4 in the table).

The calculation then proceeds as follows. Actual gross pay appears in column 2 and is cumulated in column 3. Cumulative free pay is then deducted from cumulative pay to date to give taxable pay to date in

Table C.2   An example of the cumulative principle

1	2	3	4	5	6	7
Week	Gross pay	Pay to date	Free pay to date	Taxable pay to date	Tax due to date	Actual tax due
	£	£	£	£	£	£
1	320	320	80	240	60	60
2	400	720	160	560	140	80
3	40	760	240	520	130	−10

column 5. Cumulative tax due appears in column 6 as 25 per cent of taxable pay to date. The actual tax withheld each week is the difference between the cumulative tax due and the tax withheld during the tax year so far.

One of the major benefits of this system is that it can withhold tax at source accurately throughout the year. Hence, for instance in week 3 of the table, gross pay falls below free pay, the system can even generate a rebate. See also *PAYE*.

The contrasting approach is non-cumulation which may be illustrated by the same example as in Table C.3. The main point is that each pay period is treated separately. Table C.3 shows that the non-cumulative withholding achieves the correct result in weeks 1 and 2, while the taxpayer remains subject to the same marginal rate of tax. However when the taxpayer's income falls in week 3 to £40, which is less than the free pay allowed for that week, the system cannot generate a rebate at that time because the tax paid in earlier periods is not taken into

Table C.3   An example of non-cumulative withholding

Week	Gross pay	Free pay	Taxable pay	Tax due
	£	£	£	£
1	320	80	240	60
2	400	160	560	140
3	40	240	520	130

account. Such a system will also tend to withhold too much tax if there is a progressive structure of tax rates and taxpayers' incomes rise or fluctuate during the tax year. Taxpayers are therefore pushed into higher tax brackets than would be appropriate if their position for the whole year were taken into account. With such a system, taxpayers are normally required to complete tax returns every year and any amounts overwithheld are repaid after tax liability has been formally assessed.

current year basis of assessment.   Income is charged to tax in the assessment year in which it arises. See also the *preceding year basis of assessment*.

Customs & Excise.   HM Customs & Excise is the department responsible for collecting customs and *excise duties*, *value added tax* and has certain agency functions.

customs duties.   Taxes levied on imports and exports. The customs system seems to have originated at the time of King John in the early thirteenth century. The customs levied in 1275 were export duties on wool and leather passing through certain English ports. Customs continued to be an important source of revenue because, in a primarily subsistence economy, trade was a highly visible target for taxation.

custom house.   The office at a port for the purpose of customs business.

customs union.   An arrangement between a group of countries to abolish tariffs and possibly other restrictions on trade between themselves and to maintain a common tariff wall on imports from countries outside the customs union. An example is the European Union (EU). A free trade area is a similar arrangement regarding trade between two or more countries but without the common tariff imposed on goods from outside countries.

CY.   Current year. *See current year basis of assessment.*

D

daily adjustable tax exempt securities. US bonds which can be redeemed at any time at face value plus accrued interest.

daisy-chain scheme. An arrangement designed to avoid taxation by passing a commodity through a chain of subsidiaries.

Danegeld. Originally a tax levied either to appease the Danes or to provide protection for England against them. It was a form of land tax and reached its highest yield during the reign of Ethelred. Under the Danish Canute dynasty, the levy was called heregeld.

DDP. Delivered duty paid.

DDU. Delivered duty unpaid.

deadweight loss. The loss of economic efficiency caused by a tax distorting economic behaviour. Also known as the *excess burden* of taxation.

death duties. Taxes imposed on property passing at death. There are different forms of death duty. One approach is to calculate the tax on the basis of the value of deceased's estate – as with *estate duty*. The other main type is to base the tax on the amount received by the beneficiaries – an *accessions tax* or *inheritance tax*. It has been suggested that death duties could be easy to avoid – Will Rogers commented that 'you won't catch those old boys dying so promiscuously like they did'. However the idea that wealthy individuals would avoid such taxes by giving away their wealth before they were likely to die seems to have little empirical support. Nevertheless perhaps it can still be described as a voluntary tax paid only by those who disliked their relatives more than they disliked paying tax.

debt dumping. In enterprises operating internationally, moving bad debt to a group company in a higher taxed country in order to gain the maximum tax advantage of the *write-off*.

deduction at source.   See *withholding at source.*

deductions.   Items which may be subtracted from gross income to give taxable income.

deed of covenant.   A written commitment to pay another person or an organization a specified amount of money at regular intervals for a specified number of years or until some event such as the death of one of the parties. Historically deeds of covenant could be used to transfer taxable income from one person to another. This allowed scope for tax *avoidance* by transferring income, say, to other members of the family who faced lower tax rates. In more recent years, the scope for using covenants in this way has been restricted.

deep discount bonds.   Bonds which yield little or no interest but are sold below the redemption value. Investors therefore receive a capital gain as the bond approaches its redemption date. This may be advantageous if capital gains are taxed more lightly than are interest payments.

deferred earnings.   Sometimes used to describe a pension earned during a period of employment.

deferred taxation.   Taxation attributable to differences in timing between profits recorded in financial accounts and profits established for the purposes of taxation.

deflection of tax liability.   Where an individual or company's tax liability is transferred to someone else.

delinquent tax.   Tax which should have been paid and has not been. The defaulting individual may be described as a 'delinquent taxpayer'.

de minimis.   Abbreviation for *de minimis non curat lex* – the law does not take account of trifles. In taxation it refers to some minimum level below which the normal rules will not apply. For example, in many cases a tax authority will not strive to collect small amounts of tax which fall below a certain specified level. See also *tolerances.*

democracy.   A method of government where the power resides with the people and is exercised by them either directly or by means of elected representatives. Such a political organization may have implications for the type of tax system employed.

FURTHER READING
Downs, A. (1956), *An Economic Theory of Democracy*, New York: Harper & Row.
Steinmo, S. (1993), *Taxation and Democracy: Swedish, British and American Approaches to Financinq the Modern State*, New Haven, CT: Yale University Press.

departure prohibition order. A device used in some countries to prevent a taxpayer leaving the country if their departure might enable them to escape taxation. See also *jeopardy assessment.*

departure tax. A tax on individuals leaving a country. Such taxes have a variety of names such as airport tax or embarkation tax and are normally levied as a fixed sum per person.

depletion allowances. Tax relief reflecting the loss of value as natural resources such as oil or coal are extracted and cannot be replaced.

depreciation. The fall in the value of fixed assets over time. Different tax systems take account of depreciation in different ways. In the UK it is through a system of *capital allowances.*

desk audit. A tax *audit* undertaken in the tax office.

destination principle. A principle widely incorporated into VAT legislation that tax should be paid in the country in which the goods are consumed and not in the country in which they originate. Imports are therefore subject to VAT but the tax is remitted on exports. See also *origin principle.*

deterrent taxes. Penalties for failure to comply with the tax system.

development land tax. A tax intended to capture the increase in value from changing the use of land. It was in force in the UK from 1976 to 1985 when the rate of tax was 60 per cent.

differential tax incidence. A comparison of the *incidence* of two taxes assuming total tax revenue and government expenditure remain the same. See also *absolute tax incidence.*

direct tax.   A tax assessed on and (in principle at least) collected from the individuals who are intended to bear it. It may be contrasted with an *indirect tax* which is levied on one group with the intention that it be passed on to other individuals. This classification can be traced back to John Stuart Mill who wrote:

> A direct tax is one which is demanded from the very persons who, it is intended or desired, should pay it. Indirect taxes are those which are demanded from one person in the expectation and intention that he shall indemnify himself at the expense of another,
>
> *Principles of Political Economy* (1871), bk. V, ch. III

However the analysis of the *incidence of taxation* reveals that direct taxes can be passed on through changes in wages or other variables. For instance, an increase in income tax which reduced the net return to saving might reduce the supply of capital. Part of the tax burden might then be passed on through higher gross interest rates.

disclosure.   Tax authorities normally have the power to demand information about taxpayers and their affairs - usually from both the taxpayers themselves and from other sources if appropriate.

discovery.   A word that has long formed part of tax legislation. It refers to the situation where it is found that some income was overlooked for tax or some relief was granted too generously. The result is a *discovery assessment* to tax.

discovery assessment.   An assessment to tax raised by a tax official who discovers that tax has been underpaid.

FURTHER READING
Williams, D.F. (1992), 'Discovery assessments: Cenlon, Olin and statement of practice S.P. 8/91', *British Tax Review*, 323–333.

discretionary trust.   A *trust* under which the *trustees* are given discretion as to who should benefit and by how much. Discretionary trusts have been used to reduce liability to taxation but legislation has reduced the extent to which this can be done.

disincentive effect.   The possibility that taxes might discourage some desirable activities such as work, saving or investing. See *incentives*.

disincorporation. The process by which an incorporated enterprise become unincorporated.

displacement effect. One of the possible explanations of the growth in the size of the public sector and the associated tax revenue. During a national crisis, such as war, public expenditure rises but after the crisis has passed does not fall back to the original level. Peacock and Wiseman argued that part of the reason for this was that the experience meant that individuals found higher tax levels more acceptable. See *threshold effect*.

FURTHER READING
Peacock, A. and J. Wiseman (1961), *The Growth of Public Expenditure in the United Kingdom*, London: Allen and Unwin.

disposable income. The income of a person or a household after tax has been deducted and any other receipts such as social security benefits have been added on. The term is also known as *take-home pay*.

disposal. Usually a sale, exchange or gift where such an event has implications for taxation.

distortion. A factor, sometimes taxation, which prevents a market economy from achieving economic efficiency.

distortionary tax. A tax which distorts the price mechanism by being imposed more heavily on some parts of the economy than on others. Sometimes this may be intentional, as with *sin taxes*, but otherwise it might encourage people to behave in a way that is rational only for tax reasons.

distraint. The legal seizure of assets which may be sold to recover taxes and other debts.

distribution function. One of the economic functions of government. It involves tax and expenditure decisions designed to redistribute spending power in the community. If markets were left entirely to themselves, individuals would receive income according to the amounts they could earn from the factors of production they own. If they owned no factors of production – no land or capital – and were unable to work, they would receive no income. A major part of government policy is therefore concerned with redistribution through taxation and social security. This occurs not only between individuals in different circumstances but also frequently for individuals over their lifetimes with net contributions being made during their working years and benefits being paid during periods of sickness, unemployment and old age. In terms of the amount of government revenue involved it could be argued that redistribution is the largest single function of most modern governments. See also *negative income tax, allocative function* and *stabilisation function.*

district.   A basic unit of organisation of the Inland Revenue and controlled by the district inspector.

dividends.   A payment by a company to shareholders. See also *corporation tax* and *imputation system.*

FURTHER READING
Bond, S., L. Chennells and M. Devereux (1995), 'Company dividends and taxation in the UK', *Fiscal Studies,* **16** (3), 1-18.

divorce.   As it appears that decisions relating to *marriage* might be influenced by tax considerations, it also seems possible that some decisions to divorce might be as well.

FURTHER READING
Cebula, R.J. and W.J. Belton (1995), 'Taxes, divorce-transactions costs, economic conditions and divorce rates: An explanatory empirical enquiry for the United States', *Public Finance,* **50** (3), 342–355.
James, S. (1996), 'Female household investment strategy in human and nonhuman capital with the risk of divorce', *Journal of Divorce and Remarriage,* **25** (2), 151–167.

Domesday Book.   A fascinating description of aspects of the economic life in the eleventh century which was produced at least partly for the purposes of taxation. Compiled for William the Conqueror in 1086, it provides a record of property ownership in England.

domestic corporation.   A company operating in its own country.

domicile.   There is no single definition of domicile and the concept is complicated. However it may be thought of as the country to which a person 'belongs', though this is not necessarily the one in which that person was born. It has been said that while 'residence' is where you live, domicile is where you think you live. Another approach is to interpret domicile as a person's real home in the sense of being the place where he or she always intends to return.

FURTHER READING
Lyons, T. (1993), 'The reform of the law of domicile', *British Tax Review*, 41–51.
Green, S. (1991), 'Domicile and revenue law: the continuing need for reform', *British Tax Review*, 21–30.

domicile of choice. A person may change his or her *domicile*. This would usually happen if a person emigrates to another country with the intention of never returning to the original country on a permanent basis.

domicile of origin. Under English law this is the *domicile* a person acquires from his or her parents.

double taxation. The situation where the same income is taxed twice. This can happen where income earned in a foreign country is subject to tax by both the foreign and home governments. It can also happen where the same income is subject to two taxes as in the case of the *'double taxation of dividends'*, or to the same tax twice, as in the case of the *'double taxation of savings'*.

FURTHER READING
Skaar, A.A., 'The continental shelf and tax treaties – a case study', *British Tax Review*, 189–200.
Bartlett, R.T. (1991), 'The making of double taxation agreements', *British Tax Review*, 76–85.

double taxation of dividends. Under the *classical system*, distributed profits are taxed once to corporate taxation and then to personal income tax in the hands of shareholders. See also *imputation system*.

double taxation of savings. Income taxes may be imposed on the income from which savings are made and also on the income from those savings. As John Stuart Mill described it: 'Unless ... savings are exempted from income tax, the contributors are taxed twice on what they save, and only once on what they spend', *Principles of Political Economy* 1871, bk. V, ch. II. It is one of the main arguments used in favour of an *expenditure tax*.

double taxation relief. Tax relief in respect of income which has already been taxed abroad.

douceur. A gift or a bribe. The term has been used to describe a tax concession when a work of art or similar possession is given to a public collection. ·

drawings. The amounts a sole trader or partner actually takes from his or her unincorporated business. Such withdrawals of cash or goods are irrelevant for the purposes of taxation.

DTR. *Double taxation relief.*

Duke of Westminster 'principle'. Arising from the judgment in *Duke of Westminster* v. *IRC* [1935] 19 TC 490, it is the view that, in considering tax avoidance, UK courts follow a strict interpretation of the law and look at the *form* of a transaction rather than its substance. However, there have been different interpretations of the Duke of Westminster case and on many occasions substance has triumphed over form. See also the *Ramsey principle*.

dutiable goods. Goods subject to customs or excise duties.

duty. Taxation, especially on imports, exports, manufacture or sale of goods. The term also covers taxes on the transfer of property, licences and for the legal recognition of certain documents. Examples include *countervailing duty, customs duty, death duty, estate duty, probate duty* and *stamp duty*.

duty-free zone. An area where good may be moved without incurring customs duties or other indirect taxes.

E

earmarking. Tax earmarking or tax hypothecation involves assigning revenue from a particular tax to a specific part of public expenditure. A major example consists of National Insurance contributions. An extension of the concept would allow taxpayers to assign their taxes to particular uses. There has been some debate whether earmarking would unduly constrain government or whether it might promote greater democracy if it were possible for taxpayers to vote over different spending decisions and their associated taxes rather than a single decision on the aggregate level of public spending and taxation. Earmarking arrangements are vulnerable to general public financial pressures. For example, in the UK in principle, the Road Fund was a mechanism by which vehicle and fuel taxes paid for spending on roads. However, those taxes came to be used for general purposes and the independent life of the Road Fund finished in 1937.

FURTHER READING
Bilodeau, M. (1994), 'Tax-earmarking and separate school financing', *Journal of Public Economics*, **54** (1), 51–63.
Buchanan, J.M. (1963), 'The economics of earmarked taxes', *Journal of Political Economy*, **71** (5), 457–69.
Teja, R.S. and B. Bracewell-Milnes (1991), *The Case for Earmarked Taxes: Government Spending and Public Choice*, London: Institute of Economic Affairs.
Wilkinson, M. (1994), 'Paying for public spending: Is there a role for earmarked taxes?', *Fiscal Studies*, **15** (4), 119–135.

earned income. Income earned from employment or self-employment. The term normally includes the pensions of retired employees, the pensions being considered to be deferred earnings.

earned income relief. Tax relief on *earned income* (as opposed to *investment income*). In the UK at the time of its abolition in 1973 it was granted at a rate of two-ninths of earned income. The differential treatment between earned and investment income was then continued by the introduction of *investment income surcharge* but in 1984 that was also abolished.

47

Earned income tax credit.   US tax relief directed at low income families with children.

FURTHER READING
Scholz, J.K. (1994), 'The earned income tax credit: Participation, compliance and antipoverty effectiveness', *National Tax Journal*, **XLVII** (1), 63–87.

economic incidence.   The *incidence of taxation.*

economic rent.   A payment to a *factor of production* over and above what is needed to keep it in its current use. It has therefore been argued that, if one could be devised, a tax on economic rent would not distort an economic system. See also *land tax.*

Edgeworth, F.Y. (1845–1926).   Mathematical economist who contributed to a number of aspects of taxation. His view was that 'the science of taxation comprises two main subjects to which the character of pure theory may be ascribed; the laws of incidence and the principles of equal sacrifice', *Papers Relating to Political Economy*, Vol. II, 64.

effective tax rate.   The *average rate of tax.*

efficiency.   One of the criteria by which a tax or tax reform can be assessed. An efficient tax in this sense is one which does not distort an efficient economic system. The main aspects are the extent to which a tax might create an *excess burden*, its *administrative costs* and *compliance costs*. Other criteria include *incentives* and *equity.*

EIS.   *Enterprise investment scheme.*

electronic lodgement of returns.   The facility to submit tax returns to the revenue authorities electronically.

FURTHER READING
James, S. and I. Wallschutzky (1993), 'Returns to the future: The case for electronically submitted tax returns', *British Tax Review*, 401–405.

embarkation tax.   See *departure tax.*

emoluments.   The remuneration of employees for tax purposes. It is defined by legislation as including 'all salaries, fees, wages, perquisites and profits whatsoever'. In *Shilton* v. *Wilmshurst* [1991] STC 88 at p. 91, Lord Templeman said that the term:

... embraces all 'emoluments from employment'; the section must therefore comprehend an emolument provided by a third party, a person who is not the employer ... [It] is not limited to emoluments provided in the course of the employment; the section must therefore apply first to an emolument which is paid as a reward for past services and as an inducement to continue to perform services and, second, to an emolument which is paid as an inducement to enter into a contract of employment and to perform services in the future. The result is that an emolument 'from employment' means an emolument 'from being or becoming an employee'.

See also *foreign emoluments*.

employment. It is sometimes difficult to distinguish between employment and self-employment for the purposes of taxation. In *Fall* v. *Hitchin* [1973] 49 TC 433, it was held that employment meant 'contract of service' (in contrast to a 'contract for services' which would apply to self-employment). The relevant factors had been identified by Cooke J. in *Market Investigations Ltd* v. *Minister of Social Security* [1968] 3 All ER 732 at p. 736 as follows:

a contract of service may exist even though the control does not extend to prescribing how the work shall be done ... the most that can be said is that control will no doubt always have to be considered although it can no longer be regarded as the sole determining factor; and that factors, which may be of importance, are such matters as whether the man performing the services provides his own equipment, whether he hires his own helpers, what degree of financial risk he takes, what degree of responsibility for investment and management he has, and whether and how far he has an opportunity for profiting from sound management in the performance of his task.

employment expenses. In principle, expenses incurred in securing an income should be deducted before what is left may be considered to be the 'real income' of a taxpayer. Tax systems normally have provisions for such claims but for many employees in the UK the situation is much simpler. They are not entitled to any. The arrangement under Schedule E is that expenses may only be allowed if they are 'wholly, exclusively and necessarily incurred in the performance of the duties of his employment'. This is provided under TA 1988 s 198(1), which was formerly TA 1970 s. 189(1) and originally ITA 1853 s. 51.

If the holder of an office or employment is necessarily obliged to incur and defray out of the emoluments of that office or employment the expenses of travelling in the performance of the duties of the office or employment ... or otherwise to expend money *wholly, exclusively and necessarily in the performance of those duties,* there may be deducted from the emoluments to be assessed the expenses so necessarily incurred and defrayed [author's italics].

The original reason for this very restrictive arrangement is historical. However it remains an important factor in allowing the *UK tax system* to operate without having to issue tax returns to the majority of taxpayers. Under the original system of schedules introduced in 1803, 'employments and so on' were assessed under Schedule D, except for those from the public sector which were assessed under Schedule E, where the provision for expenses claims was severely limited. The 1920 Royal Commission on Income Tax (p. 109) recommended that all employment income should be dealt with under Schedule E since it was thought that public and private employees should have the same basis of assessment. This change came about in 1924 as a result of a decision of the House of Lords which made it extremely difficult to decide who had a 'public office' and who an 'employment of profit'.

The strongest contrast is with the tax treatment of the self-employed who, in the UK, are assessed under Schedule D. In *Mitchell and Edon* v. *Ross* [1959] 40 TC 11 at p. 50, Lord Justice Harman went as far as to say:

Now it is notorious – and, indeed, a long standing injustice, that the scale of a taxpayer's allowances under Schedule E are on an altogether more niggardly and restricted scale than under Schedule D. Indeed, it has been said that the pleasure of life depends nowadays upon the Schedule under which a man lives.

See also *wholly, exclusively and necessarily.*

enterprise investment scheme.   A UK scheme granting tax relief for investment in the shares of certain unquoted trading companies. The scheme was introduced in the Budget of November 1993.

FURTHER READING
Armitage, B. (1994), 'The enterprise investment scheme', *British Tax Review*, 350–364.

enterprise zone.   An area which benefits from special support, including some forms of tax relief, designed to encourage business to locate there.

environmental tax. A tax designed to protect the environment, for example a tax on pollution. See also *carbon tax, external effect* and *pollution tax.*

error relief. See *mistake relief.*

equalisation. An arrangement applying particularly to the taxation of distributions from new investments in *unit trusts.* The income of a unit trust is added to the price of the units until the next dividend distribution. This means that investors who purchased units between distributions would be turning part of their capital investment into taxable income. To rectify this situation, unit trusts include in their distributions an equalisation factor which represents a return of capital and which is not, therefore, subject to income tax.

equal sacrifice. The principle that taxation should be levied so that individuals lose an equal amount of *utility* in taxation. If the marginal utility of income falls as income rises, it implies that taxpayers on higher incomes should pay more than those on lower incomes. However, it does not necessarily imply that the tax system should be progressive since the degree of progressivity would depend on how quickly the marginal utility of income fell. See *sacrifice approach.*

equity. Fairness. One of the criteria for assessing the merits of a tax or possible tax reform. There are two main aspects. One is the application of concepts of fairness such as *horizontal equity* or examining particular approaches such as the *ability to pay* and *benefit approaches* to taxation. The other aspect is the *incidence of taxation* which is concerned with the distribution of the tax burden across society.

equi-proportional sacrifice. The principle that taxation should be levied so that individuals lose the same proportion of their *utility.* On the assumptions made by the *sacrifice approach,* this implies that the tax system should be *progressive* so that more tax is levied on those with a lower marginal utility of income.

equivalent taxable yield. The return from a tax-free investment expressed as if it were a return from a taxable investment.

ESC. *Extra-statutory concession.*

estate duty. A tax on property left at death. The earliest taxes of this sort appear to have been levied in Egypt in the second century BC. In Britain, the earliest version dates from the introduction of *probate duty* in 1694. The modern version was enacted in 1894. It was replaced by *capital transfer tax* in 1975. This in turn was modified in 1986 to become *inheritance tax*, which has much in common with the pre-1975 estate duty. It has been claimed that such taxes are easily avoided by people passing on their wealth before it is likely to be caught by the tax. However there is evidence to suggest that this has not been a major cause of tax avoidance. The rich generally do not seem to find this a good reason to give their wealth away. Indeed it could be said that such taxes are voluntary and only paid by those who overestimate their longevity or who prefer leaving their money to the government rather than to their relatives.

estimated assessments. A revenue *assessment* based on incomplete information from the taxpayer. Such assessments may be set at a sufficiently high level in order to provoke the taxpayer to make an appeal and to disclose the required information. If the taxpayer simply pays an estimated assessment without providing the relevant information, the inspector may assume it was too low and so raise a higher assessment the following year.

estimated tax. (1) Tax payable in advance of the determination of the taxpayer's actual liability. It is sometimes known as *provisional tax*. (2) A company's calculation of its future tax liability.

ethics. A set of moral principles or the rules of conduct recognised in a particular profession and so on. Tax ethics has developed partly as an offshoot of the more general topic of legal ethics. This in turn has grown in importance for several reasons. These were highlighted in the 1974 Watergate scandal in the USA, in which almost all of those involved in the break-in and later prosecuted were lawyers. The American Bar Association now requires 'the duties and responsibilities of the legal profession' to be part of the accreditation for law schools. In taxation there are several issues. One is that tax practitioners' aims of minimising their clients' tax liabilities might not always be fully compatible with a code of professional conduct and wider moral considerations. Another issue is that ethical attitudes might affect the willingness of individuals to comply with a tax system.

FURTHER READING
Reckers, P.M.J., D.L. Sanders and S.J. Roark (1994), 'The influence of ethical attitudes on taxpayer compliance', *National Tax Journal*, **XLVII** (4), 825–836.
Ross, S. (1992), 'Tax ethics education in the United States and Australia', *Australian Tax Forum*, **9** (1), 27–49.
Wolfman, B. and J.P. Holden (1985), *Ethical Problems in Federal Tax Practice*, 2nd edn., Charlottesville: Michie Bobbs-Merrill Law Publishers, Charlottesville.
Wolfman, B., J.P. Holden and K.L. Harris (1991), *Standards of Tax Practice*, Chicago: CCH.

evasion. Tax evasion is the illegal manipulation of one's affairs with the intention of escaping tax. It is traditionally contrasted with legal *avoidance* of taxation.

FURTHER READING
Allingham, M.G. and A. Sandmo (1972), 'Income tax evasion: A theoretical analysis', *Journal of Public Economics*, **1**, 323–338.
Battachargya, D.K. (1994), 'Tax evasion and tax revenue loss: A further examination', *Public Finance*, **49** (2), 159–167.
Hansen, D.R., R.L. Crosser and D. Laufer (1992), 'Moral ethics v. tax ethics – the case of transfer pricing among multinational corporations', *Journal of Business Ethics*, **11** (9), 679–686.
Tanzi, V. and P. Shome (1993), 'A primer on tax evasion', *IMF Staff Papers*, **40** (4), 807–828.
Jung, Y.H., A. Snow and G.A. Trandel (1994), 'Tax evasion and the size of the underground economy', *Journal of Public Economics*, **54** (3), 391–402.

excess burden. The economic cost of a tax less the revenue received by the government. It arises because taxes may distort an economic system and cause taxpayers to do things that they would not otherwise do only in order to avoid taxation.

excess profits tax. A tax levied on distributed profits which are held to have exceeded some given level.

excise. Defined by Samuel Johnson in his *Dictionary of the English Language* (1755), as a 'hateful tax levied on commodities'. It was introduced in England in 1643 and, as indicated by Johnson, rapidly became unpopular as a tax on everyday items.

FURTHER READING
O'Brien, P.K. and P. Hunt (1997), 'The emergence and consolidation of excises in the English fiscal system before the Glorious Revolution', *British Tax Review*, 35–58.

excise duty. Taxes levied on goods produced for home consumption. Another definition is that they are taxes levied at the same rates on both domestically produced and imported goods. They are a form of indirect taxation and cover products such as alcohol and tobacco. See also *customs duties*.

exemptions.   Tax relief for certain persons, incomes, items or transactions.

exempt supply.   Goods which are outside a system of *value added tax*. Suppliers are not therefore required to charge their customers VAT but they cannot reclaim tax paid on their inputs, unlike *zero-rated supplies*.

expenditure tax.   A tax on consumption. A personal expenditure tax is based on each individual's consumption expenditure. In principle at least, it could be levied at progressive rates together with *personal allowances* in the same way as income tax. It need not involve a detailed calculation of everyone's spending. Figures for income are already available to the tax authorities and, at its simplest level, income minus saving equals consumption. More generally, income could be added to capital receipts and borrowing to give a person's spending power. The next stage is to deduct items such as spending on capital assets, lending and repayment of debt. The figure that is left should represent consumption expenditure. Where personal expenditure taxes have been implemented they have not proved to be a great success. It is, however, a tax which excites economists from time to time. John Revans argued for it in 1847 and John Stuart Mill did so before the Select Committee on Income Tax and Property Tax in 1861. In this century the cause has been championed by Alfred Marshall in 1917, Pigou in 1928, Fisher in 1937, Kaldor in 1955 and the Meade Committee in 1978. It is probably due for another run shortly. See also *Hobbes*.

FURTHER READING
Kaldor, N. (1955), *An Expenditure Tax*, London: Unwin University Books.
Marshall, A. (1917), The Equitable Distribution of Taxation, reprinted in A.C. Pigou
   (ed.) (1925), *Memorials of Alfred Marshall*, London: Macmillan.
Meade, J.E. *et al.* (1978), *The Structure and Reform of Direct Taxation*, London: Allen
   & Unwin for the Institute for Fiscal Studies.
Pigou, A.C. (1928), *A Study in Public Finance*, London: Macmillan.
Revans, J. (1847), *A Percentage Tax on Domestic Expenditure to Supply the Whole of the
   Public Revenue*. London: Hatchard.

expenses.   In a tax context, these are costs involved in earning income and which may, therefore, be deducted from that income before tax is calculated. Not all expenses are allowable against income. In particular expenses of a capital nature are treated differently; in *British Insulated and Helsby Cables Ltd.* v. *Atherton* [1926] AC 205 at p. 213, Lord Cave said:

> When an expenditure is made, not only once and for all, but with a view to bringing into existence an asset or an advantage for the enduring benefit of a trade, I think that there is very good reason (in the absence of special circumstances leading to an opposite conclusion) for treating such an expenditure as properly attributable not to revenue but to capital.

external effect. A cost or benefit to someone affected by, but not directly involved in, a market transaction. For example, an industry can inflict pollution on people who are not concerned in the production or consumption of the good produced. Where the externality is a cost to third parties in this way, one of the proposed solutions has been the imposition of a tax equal to the amount of the external cost. See also *Pigovian tax*.

FURTHER READING
Cordes, J.J., E.M. Nicholson and F.J. Sammartino (1990), 'Raising revenue by taxing activities with social costs', *National Tax Journal*, **XLIII** (3), 315–320.

extra-statutory concession. A relief from taxation granted by the revenue authority although there is no explicit concession in the primary legislation.

F

FA. *Finance Act.*

factor of production. The resources which are used as inputs to produce goods and services. Traditionally these have been classified as land, labour and capital but entrepreneurship has also been considered a factor of production.

factor tax. A tax on a *factor of production.* An example is a tax on labour.

family quotient system. The French system of *income splitting* which is extended to the income of children.

FASTIMS. Fast Income Matching Service. A computerised system introduced in Australia to match items such as interest payments with the information taxpayers have included in their returns.

female labour supply. A well-established result in empirical economics is that male labour market participation does not respond much to tax changes but female participation does. Taxation does not, however, appear to have much effect on the division of labour between the spouses within the family.

FURTHER READING
James, S. (1992), 'Taxation and female participation in the labour market', *Journal of Economic Psychology*, **13** (4), 715–734.

FIDs. Foreign income dividends.

field audit. A tax *audit* which is undertaken outside the tax office – at the taxpayer's premises or elsewhere.

FIFO. *First in, first out.*

file. US term for submitting or lodging a tax return with the tax authorities.

Finance Act.   The annual Act of Parliament that amends the tax system, sets tax rates and so on. It follows a Finance Bill based on a *Budget* introduced by the Chancellor of the Exchequer. Finance Acts generally are not known for their literary achievements, as indicated by the following exchange in *Briggenshaw* v. *Crabb* [1948] 30 TC 331:

> *Singleton J.* Your appeal must be dismissed. I will pass you back your documents. If I might add a word to you, it is that I hope you will not trouble your head further with tax matters, because you seem to have spent a lot of time in going through these various Acts, and if you go on spending your time on Finance Acts and the like, it will drive you silly.
> *Mrs Briggenshaw.* I will appeal to the higher court.
> *Singleton J.* I cannot stop you, if I would. The advice which I gave you was for your own good, I thought. That is all.

The term 'Finance Bill' replaced the term 'The Customs and Inland Revenue Bill' in 1894.

FURTHER READING
Jeffrey-Cook, J. (1994), 'The first Finance Act', *British Tax Review*, 365–367.

financial year.   See *year*.

fine tuning.   The use of *fiscal policy* and monetary policy to make relatively minor adjustments intended to keep the economy on course.

first in, first out (FIFO).   For tax and accounting purposes assets are presumed to be disposed of in the same order that they were acquired. See also *last in, first out*.

first year allowance.   UK term for the *capital allowance* permitted in the first year for the purchase of plant and machinery. In the past capital allowances have been as high as 100 per cent in order to encourage investment.

fisc.   The public treasury.

fiscal.   US term for *fiscal year*.

fiscal decentralisation.   The transfer of public spending and taxation from central to local government.

fiscalist 59

FURTHER READING
Bird, R.M. (1993), 'Threading the fiscal labyrinth: some issues in fiscal decentralization', *National Tax Journal*, **XLVI** (2), 343–356.

fiscal dividend. An increase in tax revenue as a result of inflation which may be used either to reduce tax rates or to increase public expenditure or some combination of the two. It is also known as *fiscal drag*.

fiscal drag. The loss of spending power in the economy which can occur when rising prices and incomes cause a progressive tax system to take an increasing proportion of national income. This happens because more income will be taxed at higher rates and the result will be a 'drag' on spending power and thus on the economy. It can be counteracted by indexing personal taxation and the use of indirect taxes based on value, such as value added tax. See also *bracket creep*.

fiscal engineering. US term for managing the finances of a firm to take full advantage of tax concessions.

fiscal federalism. US term for an arrangement for sharing tax revenue and public expenditure between different levels of government.

FURTHER READING
Strauss, R.P. (1990), 'Fiscal federalism and the changing global economy', *National Tax Journal*, **XLIII** (3), 315–320.

fiscal fog. A term for the difficulty sometimes found in reading tax literature. FOG stands for 'frequency of gobblydegook'.

FURTHER READING
James, S., A. Lewis and I. Wallschutzky (1981), 'Fiscal fog: A comparison of the comprehensibility of tax literature in Australia and the United Kingdom', *Australian Tax Review*, **10** (1), 26–36.

fiscal illusion. The idea that when the amount of tax is spread over a number of different taxes, it reduces taxpayers' perception of the total burden.

fiscalist. A person who favours the use of *fiscal policy*, rather than *monetary policy*.

fiscal neutrality. A system of taxation which does not discriminate betwoon differcnt foiiis of eculiorillc behaviour.

fiscal policy. Government policy with respect to the use of taxation and public expenditure in order to influence macroeconomic variables such as unemployment, inflation and economic growth. It may be co-ordinated with the other main instrument of macroeconomic policy – *monetary policy.*

fiscal psychology. A branch of psychology concerned with taxation and related matters.

FURTHER READING
Schmolders, G. (1959), 'Fiscal psychology: A new branch of public finance', *National Tax Journal,* **XII** (4), 340–345.
Lewis, A. (1982), *The Psychology of Taxation,* Oxford: Basil Blackwell.

fiscal stance. The government's policy regarding taxation and public expenditure and the national economy.

fiscal welfare benefits. See *tax expenditures.*

fiscal year. A 12-month period used as the basis for taxation and public expenditure. See also *year.*

fishing expedition. A revenue enquiry into a taxpayer's activities prompted by some irregularity in the accounts or return and some suspicion that all is not as it should be. It has been described as an unstructured investigation where the revenue authority does not know what it is looking for but is searching for clues as to what it should be looking for.

flat tax or flat rate tax. A tax levied at a single rate.

FURTHER READING
Feld, A.L. (1995), 'Living with the flat tax', *National Tax Journal,* **XLVIII** (4), 603–617.
Hall, R.E. and A. Rabushka (1995), *The Flat Tax,* 2nd edn., Stanford: Hoover Institution.

flypaper effect. The idea that once taxpayers' money is in the public sector, it is likely to stick to it. So, for instance, if central government gave local government an additional grant, it is more likely to stick to local government spending than if the same money had been paid directly to local taxpayers.

forcefield analysis. A concept which may be useful in understanding tax reform. Developed from the work of Lewin, it describes the situation where the pressure for change meets the *status quo*, which is supported by a variety of forces resistant to change. The optimal outcome might be identified perhaps, as in this example, as obstructed by the resistance to change. The pressure for change may eventually overcome the resisting forces. However the forces against change may remain strong enough to deflect change from the optimal position and the result is an unsatisfactory compromise. There are many cases of tax reform which appear to fit this description. One of the more spectacular examples was the introduction of the *community charge* or poll tax in Scotland in 1989 and England and Wales in 1990.

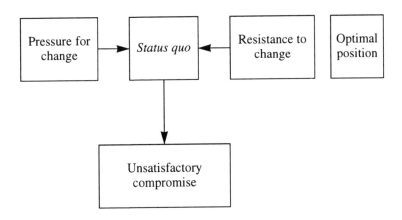

Figure F.1   A forcefield approach to tax reform

FURTHER READING
Lewin, K. (1951), *Field Theory in Social Science*, New York: Harper.

foreign diplomats. Accredited representatives of other countries who may be entitled to tax privileges.

FURTHER READING
Morris, S.N. (1991), 'The tax liability of foreign diplomats in the United Kingdom', *British Tax Review*, 207–213.

foreign emoluments. *Emoluments* of a person who is not domiciled in the UK and is paid by a non resident employer.

foreign tax credit system. US provisions for corporations to credit tax paid abroad against domestic liability.

FURTHER READING
Altshuler, R. and P. Fulghieri (1994), 'Incentive effects of foreign tax credits on multinational corporations', *National Tax Journal*, **XLVII** (2), 349–361.

form and substance. In the general area of tax avoidance, there have been differing views on whether courts should take account of the form of transactions, that is their superficial legal effect, or the substance of transactions. The *Duke of Westminster* case has been used to support the contention that it is the form that matters, whereas other cases, such as *Ramsey* have taken a wider view.

formal incidence. Where the legal obligation to pay a tax lies. It is often contrasted with *actual incidence*. See also *incidence of taxation*.

franchise tax. A tax on the right to do business in a certain jurisdiction.

franked investment income. Income received by a company, for example dividends from other UK companies, which has already borne *corporation tax*.

fraus legis doctrine. Abuse of law doctrine. A concept developed in The Netherlands which allows the authorities to disallow transactions which appear to be primarily designed to avoid tax and are outside the spirit of the legislation.

free depreciation. A system of allowing firms to choose how they write off the cost of investment expenditure for the purposes of taxation.

free pay. The amount a person can earn before becoming liable to income tax. See *cumulation* and *tax-free threshold*.

fringe benefits. Benefits from a job in addition to the wage or salary. They may include free health insurance or a company car. Fringe benefits are often not taxed as heavily as wages and salaries paid in money. Also known as *benefits in kind*.

FURTHER READING
Turner, R.W. (1989), 'Fringe benefits: should we milk this sacred cow?', *National Tax Journal*, **XLII** (3), 293–300.

fringe benefits tax. A tax on *benefits in kind*.

FTII. Fellow of the Taxation Institute Incorporated. See *Chartered Institute of Taxation*.

FURBS. Funded Unapproved Retirement Benefit Scheme. Some employers make contributions to such schemes on behalf of their employees.

Furniss v. *Dawson*. [1984] STC 153. A case which sought to clarify the conditions for applying the *Ramsey principle* and, in the process, seemed to be extending it. If a series of transactions as a whole is accepted as having a genuine commercial purpose, a particular transaction within it may still be ignored if undertaken only for the purpose of tax avoidance.

FY. *Fiscal year.*

G

gains, capital. See *capital gains tax.*

gambling tax. A tax on betting or gaming carried out for profit.

garnishee order. A legal process for recovering debts, including taxes, by requiring a third party to surrender money belonging to the debtor. A garnishee order may, for example, be imposed on an employer to withhold money in order to pay an employee's debt.

gas guzzler tax. US tax on cars with a petrol consumption rate above a particular level.

gearing. See *leverage.*

General Agreement on Tariffs and Trade (GATT). A multilateral trade treaty signed in 1947. From this GATT emerged in 1948 as an international organisation with a secretariat in Geneva. It has the aim of promoting international trade through the reduction of tariffs, import quotas and other barriers to trade. There have been successive rounds of multilateral negotiations which have made progress towards freer international trade, but there has been some slippage towards greater protectionism in some areas. The GATT has been superseded by the *World Trade Organization*, which was the culmination of the *Uruguay Round* of talks.

General Commissioners. At one time these persons were responsible for the assessment and collection of income tax but are now concerned with appeals. See *Commissioners of Income Tax.*

general sales tax. A tax levied on the sale of most goods and services.

generation skipping. A method of avoiding *transfer taxes* by putting money into trusts for beneficiaries two or more generations below the benefactor. A generation skipping tax may be used to counter such a tactic.

George, Henry (1839–1897).   US economist and known for his argument that all taxation should come from a tax on land. See *land tax*.

ghosts.   Individuals who are not known to the tax authorities but who are liable to taxation. See also *moonlighters*.

gifts *inter vivos*.   Gifts made during life.

gifts tax.   A tax on capital transfers made during life.

Gini coefficient.   A measure of the degree of inequality in income or wealth. See *Lorenz curve*.

Gladstone, W.E.   (1809–1898). British politician known later in life as the 'grand old man'. His Budget Speech of 1853 in many ways formed the basis of the modern British Budget ritual. See *Budget*.

going concern.   A business which continues to operate commercially. Such a business may benefit from *goodwill* and from certain tax relief for losses, which may not be available if the firm ceased to trade.

golden handshake.   A lump-sum payment made when a person's employment is terminated. Such payments may receive favourable tax treatment.

good faith.   Bona fides, honesty of intention; that a person believes things to be as he or she describes them. In taxation a person considered to be acting in good faith may avoid being subject to anti-tax avoidance measures.

goodwill.   A form of intangible property which is associated with the value of a business. The usual accounting definition is that it is the difference between the value of the business as a whole, as a *going concern*, and the aggregate value of its tangible and identifiable intangible assets. A rather looser definition takes it as the probability that existing customers will continue to trade with the firm even if the ownership changes.

graduated income tax.   An income tax with progressively higher rates on higher incomes. See *progressive tax*.

graduate tax.   A tax imposed on university graduates to recover part or all of the costs of their higher education paid for by the state.

green channel.   The exit at a customs post which is used by those entering a country to indicate that they are not carrying goods which exceed the customs allowances or any prohibited or restricted goods.

green dot programme.   German legislation aimed at implementing the 'polluter pays' principle. See *external cost*.

FURTHER READING
Rousso, A.S. and S.P Shah (1994), 'Packaging taxes and recycling incentives: The German green dot program', *National Tax Journal*, **XLVII** (3), 689–701.

green taxes.   Taxes designed to safeguard the environment, for example taxes on pollution. See also *carbon taxes*.

FURTHER READING
Andersen, M.S. (1994), *Governance by Green Taxes: Making Pollution Pay*, Manchester University Press.
Oates, W.E. (1995), 'Green taxes, can we protect the environment and improve the tax system at the same time?', *Southern Economic Journal*, **61** (4), 915–922.
Symons, E., J. Proops and P. Gay (1994), 'Carbon taxes, consumer demand and carbon dioxide emissions: a simulation analysis for the UK', *Fiscal Studies*, **15** (2), 19–43.
Smith, S. (1992), 'Taxation and the environment', *Fiscal Studies*, **13** (4), 21–57.
Williams, D. (1989), 'Green grow the taxes – 0!', *British Tax Review*, 396–398.

gross income.   Income before any deductions are made for expenses or other forms of tax relief.

grossing up.   When a payment is received net of tax, it is the adding back of the tax in order to calculate the original income. This may be important in a number of contexts. For example, under an *imputation system*, where an individual receives a cash dividend and a tax credit, for the purposes of taxation, the income deemed to have been received is the grossed-up figure, that is the cash dividend plus the tax credit. A different case might be where a person promised to make a payment to someone else 'free of tax', by paying the tax for them. Here the actual tax liability would be calculated on the grossed-up amount, that is the gross payment including the tax itself.

gross profits.   Sales less the costs of stock, but not taking account of the expenses of running and financing the business.

gross profits tax.   A crude tax which may be levied at low rates on gross profits.

GST.   Goods and services tax. A tax on purchases.

H

handles. See *tax handles*.

Harcourt, Sir William (1827–1904). The creator of the estate duty, the modern version of death duties, which he introduced in 1894.

hardship. In taxation, revenue authorities sometimes have the power to grant tax relief if taxpayers would otherwise face financial hardship.

harmonisation of tax. The process of removing differences between tax systems. In the increasingly extensive literature, various definitions are employed but few seem to encompass the range of meanings 'harmonisation' has acquired in a tax context. There are several possible dimensions including the taxes levied, the tax bases, the rates of tax and the ways in which taxes are administered. One approach is to derive a possible classification and this is done in Figure H.1. At one extreme there is no harmonisation at all, at the other extreme there is complete standardisation of taxes. Starting from the left of the Figure H.1, the extreme situation of no harmonisation could be mitigated by double taxation agreements and other administrative co-operation. The first substantive step towards harmonisation is for countries to have the same tax systems. Further steps are to implement the same tax bases, the same tax rates and the same methods of administration. If all those steps are taken the other extreme of harmonisation would be reached – complete standardisation. However there could be an element of decentralisation with, for instance, the rates of some taxes determined locally – described as the local government model in Figure H.1.

FURTHER READING
Daly, M. and J. Weiner (1993), 'Corporate tax harmonisation and competition in federal countries: Some lessons for the European Community?', *National Tax Journal*, **XLVI** (4), 441–461.
Fry, B.S. and R. Eichenberger (1996), 'To harmonise or to compete? That's not the question', *Journal of Public Economics*, **60** (3), 335–349.
Kopits, G. (ed.) (1992), *Tax Harmonisation in the European Community*, Washington, DC: International Monetary Fund.

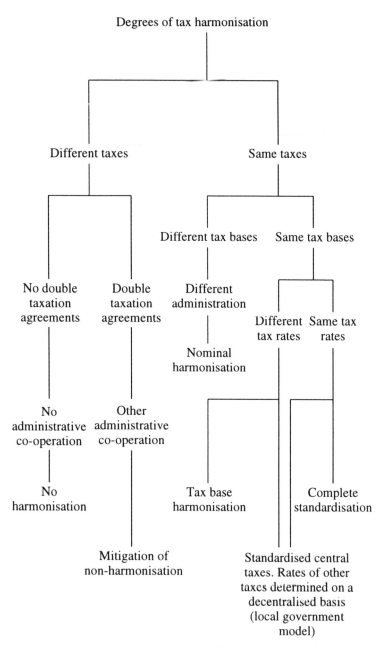

Figure H.1   Possible classification of degrees of harmonisation

havens.   See *tax havens*.

Hawley–Smoot tariff.   US *tariff* introduced in 1930 on virtually all imports in order to promote domestic production and employment. As predicted, other countries retaliated, the amount of international trade fell and the result was to worsen the Great Depression.

head tax.   See *poll tax*.

hearth tax.   A tax on hearths and stoves in England and Wales. It was abolished in 1689. See also *house tax*.

heregeld.   A continuation of *Danegeld*. It was abolished in 1051.

hidden profit distributions.   Payments made by companies to shareholders, either in cash or in the form of other benefits, but which are not described as dividends. Such benefits may be treated for tax purposes as if they were dividends, or subject to some other tax provisions.

hidden taxation.   Taxes which may not be immediately apparent to taxpayers because, for example, they may not be itemised separately in the price of goods and services.

higher rate tax.   Income tax rate(s) above the *basic rate* of tax.

hire purchase.   The process by which goods are legally hired but ownership is transferred to the hirer after a certain number of payments have been made. Where capital goods are purchased in this way and tax allowances are claimed, the capital element of the payments has to be identified.

historical cost.   The actual amount originally incurred acquiring or producing an asset. It is one method of valuing assets for tax (and other) purposes, possibly after an allowance for *depreciation*.

history of taxation.   One of life's pleasures. A great deal can be learned from the study of the history of taxation. Unfortunately this does not always happen. Hegel's view in the introduction to his *Philosophy of History*, stated that what 'experience and history teach us is this – that people and governments never have learned anything from history, or acted on principles deduced from it'. This may be a little exaggerated but the experience of the recent UK *community charge*, a version of the *poll tax*, seems to support the general point.

FURTHER READING
Dowell, S. (1884), *A History of Taxation and Taxes in England*, London: Longmans.
Webber, C. and A. Wildavsky (1986), *A History of Taxation and Expenditure in the Western World*, New York: Simon and Schuster.

Hobbes, Thomas (1588–1679).   English philosopher who is sometimes credited as the earliest proponent of a tax on consumption or expenditure rather than a tax on income. This is based on the following passage from Chapter 30 of *The Leviathan*:

> To Equall Justice, appertaineth also the Equall imposition of Taxes ... Which considered, the Equality of Imposition, consisteth rather in the Equality of that which is consumed, than of the riches of the persons that consume the same. For what reason is there, that he which laboureth much, and sparing the fruits of his labour, consumeth little, should be more charged, then he that living idley, getteth little, and spendeth all he gets; seeing that one hath no more protection from the Common-wealth, then the other? But when the Impositions, are layd upon those things which men consume, every man payeth Equally for what he useth: Nor is the Common-wealth defrauded by the luxurious waste of private men.

FURTHER READING
Hobbes, T. (1651), *The Leviathan*, London: Crooke.

hobby farmers.   Taxpayers engaged in agriculture whose objectives are not primarily commercial, but who might seek to set their losses against tax on other sources of income.

FURTHER READING
Souza, W.J. de (1991), 'The statutory trade of farming', *British Tax Review*, 15–20.

hobby trading.   An activity undertaken for personal pleasure rather than for commercial profit. Under these circumstances tax relief may not be granted in respect of any losses made. It has been suggested that revenue authorities tend to class an activity as a hobby if it makes a loss and a business if it makes a profit.

holiday.   See *tax holiday*.

horizontal equity. The idea that it is fair to treat people in similar circumstances in the similar way with respect to taxation. See also *vertical equity*.

FURTHER READING
Musgrave, R.A. (1990), 'Horizontal equity, once more', *National Tax Journal*, **XLIII** (2), 113–122.

hotel tax. A tax on hotel accommodation - usually charged to the guests.

house tax. The original tax was imposed in 1662. It consisted of a tax of two shillings on each 'firehearth or stove therein' with an exemption for less valuable houses. See also *hearth tax*.

hydrometer. An instrument used to find the relative density of a liquid and hence the strength of the mixture. For the purpose of taxation it may be used to test the alcoholic strength of drinks.

hypothecation of taxes. See *earmarking*.

I

IHT. *Inheritance tax.*

illusion, tax. The failure to appreciate that current government spending paid for by public borrowing will have to be supported by higher future tax payments

immovable property. Property such as land and buildings in contrast to movable property such as *chattels*.

impact of taxation. The initial effect of a tax on the economy. At an individual level this may be the effect on those who originally have to pay the tax. However the ultimate *incidence of taxation*, that is where the tax burden eventually falls after other economic adjustments have taken place, might be quite different.

implementation lag. The delay between a decision to alter some element of fiscal policy and its implementation. It is sometimes described as the administration lag.

implicit marginal taxation. The reduction in income-related welfare benefits as income rises. Combined with increases in direct taxation, the withdrawal of such benefits can contribute to the *poverty trap* and the *unemployment trap*.

FURTHER READING
Dickert, S., S. Houser and J.K. Scholz (1994), 'Taxes and the poor: A microsimulation study of implicit and explicit taxes', *National Tax Journal*, **XLVII** (3), 621–638.

import deposits. A form of restriction on imports with some of the features of a tax. Importers are required to deposit funds equal to a certain percentage of the value of their imports with the government. The money is returned after a period but, as an interest-free loan, it clearly adds to the costs of the importers. In the UK such a scheme was introduced in 1968 when 50 per cent of the value of most goods had to be deposited with the *Customs & Excise*, who returned the money without interest after six months. The rate of deposit was reduced a number of times and the scheme was finally ended in 1970.

import surcharge.   An addition to *tariffs*. In the UK an import surcharge was introduced on certain imports in 1964 and was removed in 1967. In the US a ten per cent surcharge was imposed on imports in 1971 but removed later that year.

import tariffs.   See *tariffs*.

impost.   A tax or duty, particularly a customs duty.

imputation system.   The system of *corporation tax* introduced in the UK in 1973 and used in some other European Union countries. It imputes to a company's shareholders all or part of the corporation tax paid by their company. The imputation is achieved by means of a *tax credit*, which is used to offset income tax liability on the dividends. An economic rationale for the system is that investment should be free to flow to those companies with the best prospects for future investment. These are not necessarily the ones making the most profits currently. If distributed profits were taxed first to corporation tax and then again to income tax in the hands of the shareholders, this might discourage distributions and thus impede the flow of money to companies with the best prospects. See also *classical system* and *split-rate system*.

FURTHER READING
Chown, J., 'International aspects of the imputation system' (1993), *British Tax Review*, 90–96.

imputed income.   *Income* a taxpayer may be deemed to have received even if that income was not in the form of cash. For example, some tax systems have taken account of the flow of benefit that taxpayers receive by living in their own homes. Income may also be imputed to a taxpayer in other circumstances.

incentives.   Taxation may affect incentives to behave in certain ways, for example, in the willingness of taxpayers to work, save and invest. Such effects can be analysed by using the concepts of *income effects* and *substitution effects*.

FURTHER READING
James, S. and C. Nobes (1996), *The Economics of Taxation*, Hemel Hempstead: Prentice Hall International.

incidence of taxation. The distribution of the burden of a tax. A contrast is often made between the impact or the *formal incidence* of taxation and the *actual incidence* of taxation. For example, indirect taxes may be formally levied on suppliers but they may be able to pass some of the burden of the tax on to their customers through higher prices. It had been thought that the burden of direct taxes, such as income tax, could not be passed on. However if the supply of labour changes as a result of the tax, part of the burden might be passed on by changes in wage rates. Tracing actual tax incidence can be quite complex since the effects of taxes can be transmitted through prices, wages and rates of interest. There are also likely to be effects on substitute and complementary goods and effects can be passed back to suppliers and forward to customers. They may also be *capitalised* by changes in capital values.

income. The flow of resources in terms of money, goods or services received over a period. There have been various other definitions by prominent economists. Haig defined income as 'the money-value of the net accretion to economic power between two points in time'. Henry Simon stated that 'personal income may be defined as the algebraic sum of (a) the market value of rights exercised in consumption and (b) the change in the value of the store of property rights between the beginning and end of the period in question'. Hicks described income as the 'maximum amount of money which the individual can spend this week, and still be able to spend the same amount *in real terms* in each ensuing week'. The economic approach therefore tends to consider income to be the accrual of wealth in whatever form. Capital gains might therefore be considered to be a form of income. Such definitions are not always easy to measure and, for this and other reasons, income taxes tend to be based on more measurable definitions of income. See also *benefits in kind* and *imputed income*.

FURTHER READING
Haig, R.M. (1921), 'The concept of income', in R.M. Haig (ed.), *The Federal Income Tax*, Columbia University Press.
Hicks, J.R. (1974), *Value and Capital*, 2nd edn., Oxford: Oxford University Press.
Parker, R.H., G.C. Harcourt and G. Whittington (1986) (eds), *Readings in the Concept and Measurement of Income*, 2nd edn., Oxford: Philip Allan.

Simons, H.C. (1985), *Personal Income Taxation: The Definition of Income as a Problem of Fiscal Policy*, Chicago: University of Chicago Press.

income averaging.   See *averaging provisions.*

income effect.   When the price of something changes there are two reasons why the amount demanded might change – the income effect and the substitution effect. The income effect refers to the part of the change caused by the change in consumers' real income, that is the amount they can buy in real terms. For instance, if the price of food rises, consumers become worse off as their spending power falls. As a result they may choose to spend less on food. The concepts of income and substitution effects are used to analyse the effects of taxation. In the analysis of income tax, the income effect is associated with changes in the *average rate of tax.* If the average rate of tax changes this will affect taxpayers' real income and it may therefore affect their economic behaviour.

income in kind.   Income which is received in the form of goods and services rather than in money. See also *benefits in kind*, which may be paid by employers as part of a remuneration package. Such income may be liable to tax.

income maintenance.   Policies designed to increase the incomes of the less well off. Such action can be affected by *implicit marginal taxation* and possible solutions include some form of *negative income tax.*

income matching.   The process of comparing the incomes that taxpayers have disclosed in their returns with other information available to the revenue authorities. The procedure has become increasingly computerised in some countries. See also *information return.*

income splitting.   (1) One way of taxing families. It involves aggregating the income of a married couple and then dividing it by half. Income tax is then calculated on each half. See also *aggregation basis of taxation.* (2) A method of reducing tax whereby a couple contrive to make it appear that some of the income earned by the spouse with the higher income is earned by the other spouse.

income tax. In principle a tax on income but in practice a tax on some incomes and not others. In economic terms *income* is usually defined as the accretion of wealth but for various practical and political reasons, income taxes are applied to something less than that. In the UK the income tax was introduced, like many taxes, to finance war. It first came into force in 1799 at the time of the war with Napoleon. The tax was repealed when peace came in 1802 but reimposed when hostilities recommenced in 1803. It was abolished once more when peace was finally achieved in 1815 but reintroduced in 1842 and has remained in force ever since. In his record breaking Budget speech of 1853, Gladstone described the income tax as 'an engine of gigantic power for great national purposes'. If you keep the tax in peace, he told the Commons, you run a surplus and acquire a 'fiscal reserve' – which is just as important as the army reserve and naval reserve. But it was above all in wartime 'when the hand of violence is let loose and when whole plains are besmeared with carnage' that 'you should have the power of resort to this mighty engine'. He also said that 'whatever you do in regard to the income tax, you must be bold, you must be intelligible, you must be decisive'. Modern income taxes are often the largest source of public revenue.

FURTHER READING
Sabine, B., *A History of Income Tax* (1966), London: Allen & Unwin.

incorporation. To form an organisation with a separate legal identity from its owners. This can have a number of commercial advantages since, if the business fails, the owners' liability is limited to their investment in the enterprise. In contrast, the owners of an unincorporated enterprise, a sole trader or a partner, would be personally liable for losses incurred. Limited liability makes it easier to raise capital. The possible disadvantages include more onerous regulatory rules which apply to incorporated enterprises. Incorporation may yield tax advantages since the profits of the business would not be liable to income tax each year in the hands of the owners. Partly for this reason such enterprises are subject to a *corporation tax*, a corporate income tax or a profits tax in many tax systems.

independent taxation. The form of the individual basis of taxation introduced in the UK in 1990. It is not a pure form, for example *married allowances* remain, but it was a major shift towards the *individual basis of taxation*.

indexation.   Linking nominal values to some index of, for example, prices, wages or real per capita incomes. In taxation, there may be provisions linking the thresholds for tax and higher rates of tax to changes in the price level thus maintaining their real values.

indirect tax.   A tax which is levied on one part of the economy with the intention that it be passed on to another. For example, value added tax is levied on the businesses involved in production and distribution with the intention that it be passed on to final consumers through higher prices. The definition was developed when it was thought that taxes could be fully passed on in this way. However it is now appreciated that at least some of the burden of indirect taxes will not be passed on. See *incidence of taxation*.

FURTHER READING
Gordon, L. (1993), 'Indirect taxes and Europe', *British Tax Review*, 164–171.

individual basis of taxation.   The principle whereby each individual is subject to taxation without regard to his or her family circumstances. See also *aggregation basis of taxation*.

individual income tax.   Income tax on individual taxpayers as contrasted with income taxes on corporations and other bodies of persons.

infant industry argument.   The argument that *tariffs* are justified to protect a new industry until it has matured sufficiently to compete with international competition. Experience would seem to suggest that it is not a very good argument for tariffs.

inflation tax.   The term inflation tax describes the fall in the value of government debt, including money, caused by inflation. In this way wealth is transferred from the holders of that debt to the government. Another way of illustrating the point is that the government can buy resources by printing more money (known as *seigniorage*) but, as this usually results in inflation, it is at the expense of those who already hold money.

informal economy.   Sometimes used as a euphemism for the *black economy*, which in turn is a euphemism for economic activity conducted outside legal requirements – particularly those relating to taxation. It can also refer to non-market economic activity.

information powers. The legal authority of a revenue service to demand information from taxpayers and third parties.

information returns. Information required by tax authorities about other individuals or companies regarding their potential tax liability. For example, banks and other institutions are often required to supply details of interest they have paid to investors. This information may then be used to check that taxpayers have been declaring their incomes in full. See also *income matching*.

informer's letter. See *anonymous letters*.

inheritance tax. In principle a tax levied on transfers on death and imposed on the heir. As with a broader *accessions tax*, which includes transfers made in life as well as on death, the amount of tax would be based on what the recipient receives. This is in contrast to an *estate duty* form of tax which is based on the total value of the donor's estate at death. In the UK, the 'inheritance tax' does not take this form. It emerged from the remains of the *capital transfer tax* in 1986. The capital transfer tax legislation was not actually repealed but substantially amended, particularly by excluding most lifetime transfers, and the result was renamed inheritance tax. As before, it is calculated on the basis of how much the donor transfers rather than on the amounts received by the donee. The arrangements are now very similar to the pre-1975 position and inheritance tax, like the old estate duty, is levied on transfers between individuals made on the death of the donor or up to seven years before death.

initial allowance. A form of tax relief relating to the *depreciation* of assets. However the aim of such an allowance is often to encourage investment. Therefore, depending on the tax system, it may be granted in the first year in addition to more specific provisions relating to the actual depreciation of commercial assets.

Inland Revenue. The body responsible for the collection of direct taxes in the UK. It was formed from the amalgamation of the Board of Stamps and Taxes and the Board of Excise in 1849. Excise duties were then administered by the Inland Revenue until they were transferred in 1909 to the Board of *Customs & Excise*.

FURTHER READING
Johnston, Sir Alexander (1965), *The Inland Revenue*, London. Allen & Unwin.

input tax.   In a system of value added tax, when an enterprise buys raw materials or other inputs, it will be charged value added tax by its suppliers. This is called input tax and represents the tax paid by the suppliers in respect of earlier stages of production. See *value added tax.*

inside lag.   The interval between the time a need for some fiscal or monetary policy action is required and its implementation.

inspectors of taxes.   Officers in the Inland Revenue responsible for the assessment of taxation. The addition of Her Majesty's to the designation of Inspectors of Taxes was a reward for their application to their work in wartime. See also *collectors of taxes* and *surveyors.*

Institute of Fiscal Studies.   An independent institute with the purpose of promoting research and informed discussion of fiscal affairs. Its address is 7 Ridgmount Street, London, WC1E 7AE.

insurance tax.   A tax on insurance cover usually charged to the insured. In some countries such a tax is imposed instead of subjecting insurance to value added tax.

FURTHER READING
Macleod, J. and P. Milnes (1996), 'Insurance premium tax', *British Tax Review*, 155–167.
Macleod, J. (1996), 'Insurance premium taxes – some international aspects', *British Tax Review*, (3), 263–271.

intangible assets.   Non-monetary assets which have no physical existence but which may be recognised as having value, for example *goodwill.*

interest equalisation tax.   A US tax designed to make the after-tax returns on foreign investments equal to the returns on comparable US securities. It was an attempt to reduce substantial capital outflows from the US but was abolished in 1974.

internal revenue.   US Government's income from federal taxes apart from customs duties.

Internal Revenue Service. The main tax authority in the US. It was set up in 1862 during the Civil War and is responsible for assessing and collecting US *internal revenue.*

interpretation of the law. The meaning attached to statutory law. See *literal interpretation of the law.*

inter vivos **gift.** A capital transfer given during the life of the donor, possibly to avoid *inheritance tax* or *estate duty.*

intestacy. The situation where someone dies without leaving a will.

intimate search. A physical search carried out at the instigation of a revenue officer of a person's body orifices for smuggled goods.

intoxicating liquor. Alcoholic beverages which legally require an excise licence before they can be sold.

investigation. A widely used term referring to the inspection of a taxpayer's financial affairs, which may vary from a simple enquiry to a thorough examination of the circumstances of the case.

FURTHER READING
Rignell, J. (1992), *How to Survive an Inland Revenue Investigation*, Plymouth: Northcote House.

investment allowances. Tax relief intended to encourage capital investment by granting tax allowances to purchasers of certain commercial assets. See *capital allowances.*

investment income. Income from investments such as dividends, interest and rent. It has been argued that investment income should bear a higher rate of tax than that imposed on income from employment. For example, one argument is that employment earnings come from a 'wasting asset' and will stop if the individual can no longer work. Another is that earnings represent the return to current toil whereas investment income represents either the return to past toil or to inherited wealth.

investment income surcharge. An additional part of *income tax* specifically applied to *investment income.* It was introduced in the UK in 1973 at the same time as *earned income relief* was abolished, so retaining a difference in the tax treatment of employment and investment income. However it was in turn repealed in 1984. It was levied on top of income tax at a rate of 15 per cent over a certain threshold. In its last year of operation it applied to investment income over £7100. It was the investment income surcharge imposed on top of normal income tax rates of up to 83 per cent which led to a top tax rate in the UK of 98 per cent in the 1970s. The highest rates of income tax were reduced in 1979.

investment trust.   A company which invests in other companies on behalf of its shareholders.

FURTHER READING
Macleod, J.S. (1994), 'Investment trusts revisited', *British Tax Review*, 111–126.

inward processing relief.   Relief from customs duties for goods imported from outside the European Union (EU) for processing before being re-exported outside the EU.

IRC.   Inland Revenue Commissioners.

IRS.   *Internal Revenue Service*.

itemised deductions.   US term for tax deductions which are listed individually, item by item. See also *standard deduction*.

J

jeopardy assessment. An assessment raised when there is a risk that the tax might otherwise be lost. For example this might happen when a taxpayer appears to try to put his or her resources beyond the jurisdiction of the tax authority. See also *departure prohibition order*.

joint assessment. A tax assessment involving the income, capital gains and so on of both a husband and wife.

joint return. A tax return made by a husband and wife together. Under some tax systems this might result in less tax being paid than if the two spouses submit separate returns.

judicial review. A procedure by which a judicial body may examine the validity of a decision of a public authority or a lower court.

FURTHER READING
Woolf, Lord (1993), 'Tax and judicial review', *British Tax Review*, 219–229.

K

Kaldor, Nicholas (1908–1986). Distinguished economist. His contributions to taxation included a notable discussion of personal expenditure tax. Kaldor was created a Life Peer in 1974.

FURTHER READING
Kaldor, N. (1955), *An Expenditure Tax*, London: Allen & Unwin.

KATE. Key Abnormal Tax Agent Evaluation. An Australian computerised system allowing the tax office to identify tax agents who complete clients' returns significantly differently from returns prepared by other agents. This may provide evidence of some systematic irregularity being repeated by a particular agent. In addition, further investigations can be undertaken of employees' tax returns, particularly since these are now categorised into quite specific occupational codes, as shown in Table K.1.

Keith Committee. A committee set up in 1980 under the chairmanship of Lord Keith to look into the question of tax enforcement. It made a number of proposals for tightening up the process of tax administration in the UK.

FURTHER READING
Committee on the Enforcement Powers of the Revenue Departments (1983), *Report*, Cmnd 8822, London: HMSO.

Kennedy Round. The sixth round of multilateral negotiations between signatories to the *General Agreement on Tariffs and Trade* (GATT). The Kennedy Round began in 1964 and finished in 1967. Its aim was to achieve straight percentage tariff reductions across the whole range of trade rather than dealing with particular areas individually. Significant success was achieved in this respect in the following years. The Kennedy Round was followed by the *Tokyo Round* and the *Uruguay Round* of negotiations.

Keogh plan. US provision which allows the setting up of a tax sheltered investment retirement plan for self-employed persons and certain

Table K.1   Examples of the occupation codes for tax purposes

Occupation	Code
Accountant	2701
Accounting machinist	5203
Accounts clerk	5301
Actor	2817
Actuarial clerk	5305
Actuary	2909
Administrative clerk	5999
Stripper	2813
Student nurse	3401
Studio hand	8999
Sub-editor	2807
Sugar cane grower	1401
Supply and distribution manager	1307
Surfer	3920
Surgeon (other)	2303
Surgeon (tree)	4805
Wood processing machine operator	7413
Wood turner	4901
Wool buyer	3913
Wool classer	3999
Word processing operator	5105
Yachtsman	3929
Youth worker	3901
Zoologist	2107

employees without company pensions. In Canada they are called Registered Retirement Savings Plans (RRSP).

Keynes, John Maynard (1883–1946). One of the most influential economists with a primary contribution on the role of government in influencing macroeconomic variables, in particular the level of employment. From this developed a huge literature on the role of taxation in stabilisation policy. Keynes was created a viscount in 1942. See also *stabilisation function*.

FURTHER READING
Keynes, J.M. (1936), *The General Theory of Employment, Interest and Money*, London: Macmillan.

kiddie tax.   US tax extended to the investment income of children. The intention was to remove the ability for parents to avoid tax by moving some of their investments to their children.

L

labour supply. Taxation may affect labour supply, for example through *income and substitution effects*. An enormous amount of empirical work has been undertaken into this topic. The general conclusion is that, overall, taxation on its own does not make a great deal of difference to how much work is done, though married women may be an exception. Musgrave has also suggested the possibility of a *spite effect*. See also *backward bending supply curve of labour* and *female labour supply*.

FURTHER READING
Brown, C.V. (1983), *Taxation and the Incentive to Work*, 2nd edn., Oxford: Oxford University Press.
Pencavel, J., 'Labor supply of men: A survey' and M.R. Killingsworth and J.J. Heckman, 'Female labor supply: A survey' (1986), in O. Ashenfelter and R. Layard (eds), *Handbook of Labor Economics*, North Holland, 3–102 and 103–204.

Laffer curve. Named after Arthur Laffer, it is an illustration of the old idea that increasing the rates of tax leads to an increase but then a decrease in total tax revenues and that there is some rate of tax at which total tax revenue is maximised. In the diagram, zero tax rates clearly yield zero tax revenue. As tax rates are increased so total tax revenue is increased until, at some tax rate *t*, tax revenue is maximised at *M*. After that point disincentive and other effects such as evasion predominate and further increases in tax rates lead to a decline in tax revenue. Arthur Laffer was an economic adviser to President Reagan in the 1980s and prominent in the *supply-side* school of economic thought.

lags. The delays in the response of some element of fiscal policy to a change in the economy. The recognition lag describes the delay before the need for action is appreciated, the implementation lag refers to the time taken to implement changes and the response lag to the time the economy takes to react.

landfill tax. A levy on the disposal of waste in, for example, tips and old quarries, introduced in the UK in 1996.

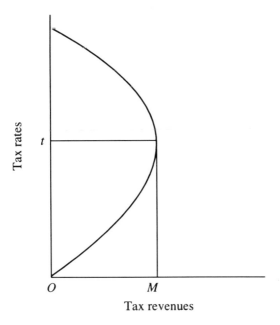

Figure L.1   The Laffer curve

land tax. A tax on land can take the form of a tax on the value of land, on the size of land holdings or on the income from land. It has been argued by *Henry George* and others that land should form the main tax base. One of the reasons is the argument that the income from land is a pure *economic rent*, that since land will not disappear from use, taxing it will not distort economic behaviour. It has also been argued that the value of land is largely determined by the community as a whole and therefore some of this should be returned to the community through taxation. See also *development land tax*.

FURTHER READING
George, H., *Progress and Poverty* (1882), New York: Appleton.

last in, first out (LIFO).   A method of stock valuation which uses the cost of the most recently purchased stocks of raw materials and finished goods. Such stocks can therefore be valued at current prices. See also *first in, first out*.

Layfield Report.   The Report of the Committee of Inquiry into Local Government Finance in the UK. An important inquiry into *local government finance*. It considered that there should be clear accountability for local government expenditure, that those responsible for spending the money should also be responsible for raising it. It presented two alternative approaches. One was the 'central solution' whereby central government would be responsible for most local expenditure and also for providing resources. The Committee preferred the second alternative, in which local authorities should be primarily responsible for local expenditure. If local autonomy was to be achieved, local authorities would require additional sources of revenue and the Committee thought that a *local income tax* was the only realistic solution. In a note of reservation a third possibility was proposed. This argued that central government would be responsible for maintaining minimum standards of local services but that local authorities would be permitted to provide higher standards from local sources of revenue.

FURTHER READING
Layfield, F. (1976), Chairman, *Local Government Finance: Report of the Committee of Enquiry*, Cmnd 6453, London: HMSO.

lease.   A contract whereby the lessee hires a specific asset from the lessor who retains ownership of the asset. There can be tax advantages in leasing an asset instead of buying it. For example, the lessor might be able to make better use of tax provisions for *depreciation*. Part of the benefit may then be passed on to the lessee through lower lease payments.

least aggregate sacrifice.   The variation of the *sacrifice approach* which suggests that each taxpayer should give up the same amount of utility in taxation. This implies that individuals with a low marginal utility of income should pay more tax than those with a higher marginal utility of income.

leverage.   US term for 'gearing' but becoming more commonly used in the UK. It describes the relationship between the funds provided by shareholders in an enterprise and funds requiring a fixed return, such as bonds and preference shares.

FURTHER READING
Briffett, R. (1990), 'Leverage and the changing concept of adequate capitalisation' *British Tax Review*, 12–35.

levy. A form of taxation. Originally it referred particularly to a tax raised for a specific purpose and charged at a given rate per taxpayer. In former times it has also been used in respect of fines, but now is often synonymous with taxation.

lien for taxes. As part of its tax collection procedures, a tax authority may attach a lien (legal claim) on the property of a person who owes taxes.

lifetime incidence analysis. The analysis of the distribution of the tax burden over taxpayers' lifetimes.

FURTHER READING
Fullerton, D. and D.M. Rodgers (1993), *Who bears the Lifetime Tax Burden?* Washington, DC: Brookings Institution.

LIFO. *Last in, first out.*

limited liability. A legal arrangement such that should a limited liability company fail, the shareholders' liability is limited to the amount of capital they have invested.

linear tax system. A tax system which consists of a tax-free allowance whereby income in excess of this allowance is subject to a single rate of tax. In the Figure L.2, taxpayers could receive up to *OT* in income before tax is levied. Above *T* all additional income is subject to the same *marginal rate of tax.* The single rate of tax has led some to suppose that this is a *proportional tax.* This is not so. After the tax threshold *T* is reached, although the marginal tax rate remains the same, the average rate of tax rises as income rises. This means that the proportion of income taken in tax rises as income rises and it is therefore a *progressive tax.* However, it is true that it is less progressive than a tax levied at a series of higher marginal rates.

liquor taxation. See *alcohol taxation.*

literacy. See *tax literacy.*

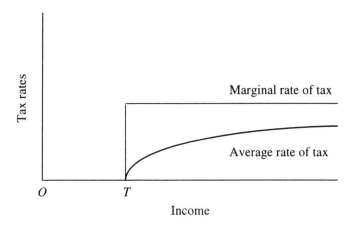

Figure L.2   Linear tax schedule

literal interpretation of the law.   Law should be interpreted literally without reference to other matters. It is sometimes found in extreme form, for example as stated by Lord Cairns in *Partington* v. *Attorney-General* [1869] LR 4 HL 100 at p. 122:

> If a person sought to be taxed comes within the letter of the law he must be taxed, however great the hardship may appear to the judicial mind to be. On the other hand, if the Crown, seeking to recover the tax, cannot bring the subject within the letter of the law, the subject is free, however apparently within the spirit of the law the case might otherwise appear to be.

A further authority sometimes cited on the point is Rowlatt, J. in *Cape Brandy Syndicate* v. *IRC* [1921] 1 KB 64 at p. 71:

> In a taxing Act one has to look merely at what is clearly said. There is no room for any intendment. There is no equity about a tax There is no presumption as to a tax. Nothing is to be read in, nothing is to be implied. One can only look fairly at the language used.

See also *Pepper* v. *Hart.*

local government finance.   The ways in which local authorities, whether city, district or region, can be financed. They could be financed by direct grants from central government. However it has been argued that local authorities should not be too reliant on central funding. This might reduce their independence, reduce local choice regarding local levels of public expenditure and make them less accountable to local taxpayers. There may be some scope for charging for local authority services but this may be limited by the nature of these services, for example it is not easy to charge for the provision of local *public goods*. This leaves local taxation. In considering which might be the best local taxes the normal criteria for taxation apply – *efficiency, equity* and *incentives*. However there are some additional criteria for good local taxes. One is that the tax base must be substantial and spread relatively evenly across different local authorities. Another is that, if local areas are to be able to exercise some choice in the level of local spending, the tax should be capable of being levied at different rates in different areas. See also the *Layfield Report* and the *Tiebout model*.

local income taxes.   Local income taxes are used to finance local government in many countries. They have the advantage of being related to *ability to pay*.

local sales tax.   A possible form of *local government finance*. It has the disadvantage that, if it is levied at different rates in different local authority areas, taxpayers in high tax areas will have an artificial incentive to shop in low tax areas.

locked-in.   An individual is said to be locked into an asset if the sale of that asset would trigger a liability to tax. This may happen when a tax is levied on a *realisations basis* as is usual with *capital gains tax*. It is less likely to happen when a tax is levied on an *accruals basis*.

lodge.   Australian term for submitting or filing a return with the tax authorities.

London provincial districts.   A considerable amount of the tax work has been moved out of London to London provincial districts located in cities such as Bradford, Edinburgh and Glasgow. This has been done for a number of reasons including the difficulty of recruiting suitable staff in London and to assist the government's regional economic policy. If a London taxpayer, who is dealt with by one of these districts, wishes to have an interview in London, it can still be arranged locally.

long service award. An award to an employee for long service, that is over 20 years, may be tax-free if it falls within certain quite restrictive limits.

Lorenz curve. A graphical analysis which is used to describe the degree of inequality of income or wealth and has therefore been used to assess the effect of taxation in this respect. It is named after the statistician, Max Otto Lorenz. The Lorenz curve is derived by taking the proportion of income (or wealth) received by the top percentile of the population, the proportion received by the next percentile and so on through the population. An example is given in Figure L.3. If everyone had the same income, the Lorenz curve would follow the line 45° of complete equality. This would show that the top 5 per cent of the population received 5 per cent of the income, the top 10 per cent received 10 per cent of the income and so on. The further the Lorenz curve is from that line the greater the inequality. This can be calculated using the *Gini coefficient*. This measures the area between the line of

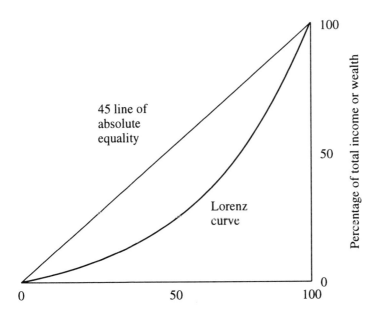

Figure L.3   The Lorenz curve

complete equality and the actual Lorenz curve as a proportion of the total area under the line of complete equality. If there were complete equality, the value of the Gini coefficient would be zero and the greater the inequality the greater the value of the coefficient. This is not a very precise measure since it cannot take account of the precise shape of the Lorenz curve, only its average distance from the line of absolute equality.

loss relief.   Income tax systems usually contain provisions which allow enterprises to deduct losses before calculating a figure for income. For various reasons, in economic terms, loss relief may not always be received in full. This might be because a firm goes out of business before it has made any profits to set the losses against. It might be that in good years the profits are taxed at progressively higher personal income tax rates while in bad years the losses are set against profits which would otherwise have been taxed at lower rates.

lottery.   See *national lottery*

lottery tax.   A tax on lotteries which may take the form of a levy on prizes, or on the sale of lots, or on the organisers of the lottery.

lump-sum allowance.   A tax allowance granting a certain sum in respect of expenses, regardless of whether or not that amount was actually incurred in expenses.

lump-sum tax.   A tax of the same amount regardless of the taxpayers' circumstances and behaviour. Its main manifestation has been in economic analysis where it is used as an example of a tax which does not cause an *excess burden* and so is economically efficient. In practice it is difficult to find examples of such a tax. One of the nearest is a *poll tax* which took the form of the *community charge* in the UK. However such taxes do not score well in terms of equity and can incur considerable unpopularity.

luncheon vouchers.   Something of a historical relic. Vouchers supplied to employees which cannot be exchanged for cash. Provided they do not exceed a value of 15 pence a day, a figure which has not been increased for many years, they are tax-free. Luncheon vouchers worth more than 15 pence are taxable as a *benefit in kind* on the excess.

luxury taxes. Taxes which are directed at 'luxury' or 'non-essential' items. It has been thought that such taxes might be relatively painless because they would be levied on purchases which could easily be foregone and would tend to be paid by more wealthy taxpayers. Neither of these assumptions may be true in practice. It is not always easy to define 'luxuries' in this context and some goods which might be so considered, such as tobacco, are not easily foregone by many consumers. Secondly the assumption that such taxes necessarily fall more heavily on the rich neglects the analysis of the *incidence of taxation*. A tax on luxuries may fall on wealthy consumers, but it is also possible that such goods and services are produced by relatively poorer people and such a tax would affect them as well.

LVO. Local VAT office.

M

machine bingo. A gaming machine used to play bingo and requiring a gaming machine licence from *Customs & Excise*.

Magna Carta. Also known as Magna Charter. A *charter* of personal and political liberty obtained by the barons from King John in 1215. Among other things, it restricted taxation. See also *taxpayers' charter*.

main residence. In some tax systems a person's only or main home is treated favourably for tax purposes. It is sometimes known as the principal residence.

mainstream corporation tax. The part of a company's *corporation tax* liability which remains to be paid after any payments of *advance corporation tax*.

maintenance payments. Payments made to a former spouse or to maintain certain relatives. They may be taken into account for tax purposes. See also *alimony*.

maladministration. Inefficient or improper administration, used particularly with reference to government departments. See *ombudsman*.

mandatory contributions. Sometimes used to describe social security contributions.

marginal rate of tax. The rate of tax on an additional unit of the tax base. For example, in the case of income tax, it is the rate of tax levied on one extra pound or dollar received. For this reason it may affect economic behaviour by changing the net money rewards to work, saving, enterprise and so on. This is known as the *substitution effect* of taxation. Taxpayers' behaviour may also be affected by the *average rate of tax*.

marginal relief. Under some tax structures when income (or sometimes capital) exceeds the tax-free limit, tax becomes payable on the whole amount. As this might mean that a small increase in income or capital could lead to a large increase in taxation, marginal relief may be available for cases where the income or capital only slightly exceeds the threshold for tax.

marriage.   There has been a great deal of debate about the taxation of marriage. Historically married couples have normally been treated differently from single people for tax purposes. This results in the *aggregation basis of taxation* whereby a couple's income is aggregated for the purposes of taxation and there may be a special *married allowance*. The result is that taxation may fall less heavily on married than on unmarried individuals. The opposite approach is to ignore marriage for the purpose of taxation and adopt an *individual basis of taxation*. In the UK a major move in this direction was made with the introduction of *independent taxation* in 1990. There are various arguments regarding these two approaches. One is that marriage alters a person's taxable capacity. If a person supports his or her spouse financially this may lower taxable capacity. On the other hand marriage may generate non-pecuniary income. For instance, when a single person pays someone for housekeeping and similar services, the transaction passes through the market and is subject to tax. In marriage such services between partners are not taxed and so, the argument runs, marriage may result in a higher taxable capacity. Clearly very different views can be held on such matters. The possibility that marriage itself may be the subject of taxation has caused some amusement. In one of A.P Herbert's famous cases it was speculated that:

> Marriages, like intoxicating liquors, might be graded according to their strength; and the most passionate, happy, or fruitful couples could be made to pay more than the lukewarm or miserable!

FURTHER READING
Alm, J. and L.A. Whittington (1995), 'Does the income tax affect marital decisions?', *National Tax Journal*, **XLVIII** (4), 565–572.
Gelardi, A.M.G. (1996), 'The influence of tax law changes on the timing of marriages: A two country analysis', *National Tax Journal*, **XLIX** (1), 17–30.
James, S. (1987), 'The reform of personal taxation', *Accounting and Business Research*, **17** (Spring), 117–124.

married allowance.   An additional tax relief given to one or both partners in a marriage.

maximum tax. A progressive income tax combined with a personal wealth tax could impose a very high rate of tax on some individuals and therefore a maximum rate of combined taxation is applied in some countries.

McKenna duties. Protective import duties introduced in 1915 by Reginald McKenna as Chancellor of the Exchequer.

Meade Report. An influential report of the findings and recommendations of a committee chaired by James Meade, who was awarded the Nobel Prize in Economics in 1978. It was originally envisaged that the Committee would examine the UK tax system as a whole, produce a statement of the objectives of taxation and make recommendations for reform – all within a year. In the event this could not be done and the Committee restricted its scope to direct taxation only and took two years – a feat described as a 'remarkable achievement' by the Director of the sponsoring *Institute for Fiscal Studies*. The Committee favoured a move towards a progressive personal expenditure and some form of progressive tax on wealth which discriminates against inherited wealth.

FURTHER READING
Meade, J.E. *et al.* (1978), *The Structure and Reform of Direct Taxation*, London: Institute for Fiscal Studies and Allen & Unwin.

meal vouchers. Sometimes supplied by employers to their staff where there are no staff meals' facilities. They may therefore be treated as a *benefit in kind* and treated as income for the purpose of taxation. See also *luncheon vouchers.*

means tested benefits. Social security benefits which are related to individuals' incomes. As incomes rise, such benefits are withdrawn and may interact with the tax system to generate a *poverty trap.*

medical expense. An item which may be deducted in the calculation of taxable income in many tax systems. This is not usually so in the UK. In a widely quoted judgment relating to the medical expenses of a professional shorthand writer, Lord Green stated:

> True it is that if you do not get yourself well and so incur expenses to doctors you cannot carry on your trade or profession, and if you do not carry on your trade or profession you will not earn an income, and if you do

not earn an income the Revenue will not get any tax. The same thing applies to the food you eat and the clothes you wear. But expenses of that kind are not wholly and exclusively laid out for the purposes of the trade, profession or vocation. They are laid out in part for the advantage and benefit of the taxpayer as a living human being. *Norman* v. *Golder* [1945] 1 All ER 352 at p. 354.

microeconomics.   The study of the economic behaviour of individual units of an economic system, especially households and firms.

FURTHER READING
Blundell, R. (1995), 'Tax policy reform: Why we need microeconomics', *Fiscal Studies*, **16** (3), 106–125.

military service exemption tax.   A levy payable by Swiss nationals who are exempted from military service.

Mill, John Stuart (1806–1873).   Major philosopher and political economist. His *Principles* include a range of taxation issues including general principles and the classification of taxes into 'direct' and 'indirect'.

FURTHER READING
Mill, J.S. (1848), *Principles of Political Economy*, London: J.W. Parker.

mineral royalties.   Sometimes payable to the government of the country in which the minerals were extracted.

minimum aggregate sacrifice principle.   The principle that taxation should be taken from those who derive the least utility from money. See *sacrifice approach*.

minimum tax.   In some tax systems *corporations* are subject to a minimum level of tax regardless of the level of their profits.

MIRAS.   Mortgage interest relief at source. The UK mechanism by which income tax relief is given to borrowers of a mortgage loan. The relief is given via the lender. This has the benefit of avoiding the administrative burden of dealing with the relief separately for each borrower.

mistake relief.   Tax relief which may be granted where tax was over-assessed because of an error or omission from a return or statement.

This does not always apply and there may be a time limit on valid claims.

mixed use property. Property which is used partly for business and partly for private purposes.

mobile telephones. A modern target for taxation. In his 1991 Budget speech, the Chancellor of the Exchequer, Norman Lamont stated:

> I turn now to one of the great scourges of modern life: the mobile telephone. I propose to bring the benefit of car phones into income tax and simplify the tax treatment of mobile phones by introducing a standard charge on the private use of such phones provided by an employer ... I hope that as a result of this measure, restaurants will be quieter and roads will be safer.

monetary policy. One of the two main policies available to the government to influence the overall level of economic activity, the other being *fiscal policy*. Monetary policy is usually operated through measures to control the supply of money and the availability of credit or to influence the level of interest rates.

money box companies. Offshore subsidiary companies in which surplus funds of the parent company can be invested in a more favourable tax climate.

monopolies, taxes on. A monopoly is a single seller of a good or service, and economic analysis suggests that a monopoly can make extra profits by limiting sales and thus keeping prices high. Historically monopolies have been granted by the monarch in order to raise revenue, and the tobacco monopolies of some European countries were originally set up to enable the government to tax the resulting profits.

moonlight economy. That part of the economy which uses cash, partly at least so that there are no records of transactions which might become known to the tax authorities. See also *black economy*.

moonlighters. Individuals who are known to the tax authorities but who have undeclared additional income. See also *ghosts*.

mortgage. A legal arrangement whereby the ownership of an asset is used as security for a loan.

mortgage interest relief.   A tax relief on interest on a loan used to buy a home. In the UK it is largely administered through *MIRAS*. Depending on the purpose of the relief there is some doubt if it achieves its objectives. For example, if the aim is to encourage people to buy their own homes, this may be frustrated by the *capitalisation* effect of taxation. In this case, by making it cheaper to borrow to buy homes, the demand and therefore the price of homes may rise. The benefit of the relief therefore tends to accrue to existing home owners rather than to new ones.

FURTHER READING
Woodward, S.E. and J.C. Weicher (1989), 'Goring the wrong ox: A defence of the mortgage interest deduction', *National Tax Journal*, **XLII** (3), 301–313.

multilateral tax treaties.   Treaties between three or more countries to avoid double taxation on income and capital. They may also include agreements about the exchange of information and the control of tax evasion. See also *unilateral relief*.

multinational enterprise.   A business producing goods and services in more than one country.

multi-stage tax.   A tax levied at some or all stages of production. See *cascade taxes*.

municipal bond fund.   US term for a mutual fund which invests in tax-free municipal bonds.

municipal bonds.   A security issued by a state or a city, the interest from which may be tax-free.

municipal taxation.   See *local government finance*.

mutual fund.   US term for *unit trust*.

N

national heritage. Items such as works of art may be treated leniently for the purposes of taxation in some countries.

National Insurance contributions. A form of social security taxation. In the UK National Insurance contributions are levied under four different classes.

Class 1 contributions are payable by employees and their employers according to the level of earnings.

Class 2 contributions are levied at a flat rate on self-employed individuals.

Class 3 contributions are voluntary and are designed to allow an individual to build up sufficient contributions to secure the state retirement pension.

Class 4 contributions are payable by self-employed individuals and the amount is determined by the level of profit as determined for income tax purposes.

national lottery. If conducted by, or on behalf of, government a national lottery is sometimes referred to as a type of tax. This is partly because such lotteries are often used to pay for public expenditure which would otherwise be paid out of taxation and partly because the odds are against winning. As Adam Smith wrote in his book *The Wealth of Nations* in 1776 (bk. I, ch. X): 'Adventure upon all the tickets in the lottery, and you lose for certain; and the greater the number of your tickets the nearer you approach this certainty'. See also *lottery tax.*

negative excess burden. The economic gain where a tax is used to correct some distortion in the economy. It is therefore the opposite of an *excess burden* where the tax itself distorts the economy. An example of a tax which may have such a beneficial effect might be an *environmental tax.*

negative income tax. A form of *income maintenance* in which social welfare payments are viewed as a negative tax payment.

FURTHER READING

Tobin, J., J.A. Pechman and P. Mieszkowski (1967), 'Is a negative income tax practicable?', *Yale Law Journal*, **77** (1), November, 1–27.

negative interest tax.   A tax which has been imposed in Switzerland on new bank accounts held by foreigners when the balance exceeds a particular amount.

neglect.   Failure to fulfil one's legal obligations in respect of taxation. It can attract penalties.

net income.   Gross income less allowable expenses.

net profits.   Gross profits less allowable business expenses.

net wealth tax.   A wealth tax based on assets less liabilities. See *wealth tax*.

Neumark Committee.   A Committee set up by the European Commission under the chairmanship of Fritz Neumark to examine tax harmonisation. Its findings are to be found in EEC Commission (1963), *The EEC Reports on Tax Harmonization*, Amsterdam: International Bureau of Fiscal Documentation.

neural network software.   A type of artificial intelligence. It has been reported that the Internal Revenue Service has been testing neural network software developed by nuclear weapons' scientists at the Los Alamos National Laboratory in New Mexico. The aim is to see if it can detect fraud in electronically filed tax returns by identifying patterns in returns submitted under different names but prepared by the same person using consistently fraudulent techniques.

neutrality.   Refers to taxes which do not affect economic behaviour. See also *excess burden*.

New Beveridge Scheme.   A scheme considered by the *Meade Committee* which would involve the further implementation of the 1942 Beveridge Report. The scheme would include the co-ordination of the income tax and social security systems and, in particular, tax thresholds and National Insurance benefits would be increased in line with the minimum acceptable standard of living.

NIC. *National Insurance contributions.*

nominee. The legal owner of an asset but who owns it on behalf of someone else – the beneficial owner.

non-cumulation. A system of withholding tax at source in such a way that the amount of tax withheld in any week or month of the tax year is based on the income received in that period less the appropriate fraction of the annual allowances and deductions, but without reference to the income received or tax paid in preceding periods. See also *cumulation.*

non-profit organisations. Organisations which do not aim to make profits. Under many tax systems they may benefit from special tax arrangements.

FURTHER READING
Beer, Y. (1995), 'Taxation of non-profit organisations: Towards efficient tax rules', *British Tax Review*, 156–172.

non-resident. A person who is not *resident* or *ordinarily resident* in the country.

non-standard tax reliefs. Tax relief which is determined by the actual expenses incurred by taxpayers, rather than a lump-sum allowance.

non-tariff barriers. Impediments to international trade other than *tariffs.* These may include quality standards and other regulations imposed by some countries.

non-taxable dividend. US term for money paid to shareholders as returns or as capital. For tax purposes the cost of the securities must be reduced by the amount of the 'dividend'.

non-taxable income. Income which is not subject to taxation and is therefore normally disregarded in the calculation of taxable income.

Nordic conventions. Multilateral agreements between Denmark, Finland, Iceland, Norway and Sweden for the avoidance of double taxation on income and capital.

No taxation without representation.   The principle that tax should not be levied unless the taxpayer has some influence on the decision, usually through elected representatives. A more recent version by J.B. Handelsman, noting the likelihood of tax evasion, is that 'there can be no taxation without misrepresentation'.

nothings.   A term used to describe intangibles such as *goodwill*.

notice of assessment.   A written statement informing the taxpayer of his or her tax liability.

notice of coding.   The document issued in the UK to inform a taxpayer of his or her tax-free income. This figure is represented as a code number which is used to calculate the amount of tax which should be withheld at source by the *PAYE* system.

NRE.   Net relevant earnings.

NTB.   *Non-tariff barrier.*

nuisance duty.   An import duty which raises less revenue than the cost of collecting it.

O

offers by taxpayers. Where *back duty* is involved taxpayers may make an offer to the Inland Revenue in respect of a full settlement of tax liability, interest and penalties. In such cases, a relevant consideration may be that the taxpayer has co-operated fully with the authorities.

office. The classic definition is that of Rowlatt J. in *Great Western Railway Company* v. *Bater* [1920] 8 TC at 231 at p. 235: was that an office or employment was 'a subsisting, permanent, substantive position, which had an existence independent from the person who filled it, which went on and was filled in succession by successive holders'. This definition has been modified by the House of Lords in *Edwards* v. *Clinch* [1981] STC 617 at p. 619. In that case it was held that an office involves 'a degree of continuance (not necessarily continuity) and of independent existence; it must connote a post to which a person can be appointed, which he can vacate and to which a successor can be appointed'. In other words continuity is no longer necessary though the office must be capable of continuance.

official error. An error on the part of the revenue authority. Under certain circumstances some or all of the tax involved may be remitted.

official insolence. A colourful description of tax administration unhindered by courtesy.

FURTHER READING
Stebbings, C. (1996), 'One hundred years ago: "official insolence"'. *British Tax Review*, 184–185.

official seal. A seal affixed by or at the order of a revenue authority and which may be removed only with its permission.

offshore funds. Investment schemes operated abroad, usually to avoid UK taxation. They are similar to unit trusts but are not regulated by the Department of Trade and Industry.

Ombudsman. The Parliamentary Commissioner for Administration. The idea and the name come from Sweden. In the UK, the Ombudsman may be approached through a Member of Parliament and asked to investigate alleged maladministration in government departments. Revenue departments generate a significant proportion of complaints but they involve only a tiny percentage of the total number of taxpayers. It might also be added that the problem does not always lie with the revenue service itself. For example, in his second report for 1976, paragraph 7, the Ombudsman wrote:

> The complexities of tax law, coupled with the need for official explanations to be factually accurate tend to encourage the use by tax offices of a 'tax language' that is often difficult for the average taxpayer to understand unless he is supported by professional advice. Indeed, I sometimes find it difficult to avoid 'tax language' in my own reports. My impression is that some complainants put their cases to me for investigation, not so much because they can point to any particular action which they regard as maladministration causing them to suffer injustice, but because they have not really understood the explanations (including some fairly complicated arithmetical computations) which they have been given.

open market value. The price an item might be expected to fetch if sold freely on a market in which anyone may participate.

optimal tariff. A *tariff* designed to maximise a country's prosperity. The argument is that if a country is a large enough buyer or seller of a product it may be able to gain an advantage by manipulating the market. For example, if a country were able to reduce the world price of a good by restricting its imports, it would then be able to buy at a lower price. It might be possible to do this with a tariff. It might also work if the country had a monopoly on the production of a good or raw material. By restricting its exports, it could push up the world price and increase its profits. Such a strategy, of course, might lead to retaliatory action by other countries.

optimal taxation. A tax structure designed to take account of both the requirements of economic efficiency and the need to be fair between one taxpayer and another. To some extent there is a trade-off between the two criteria. A tax system which is economically efficient may not be considered fair and vice versa. The purpose of the optimal taxation literature is to find the best balance between the two.

FURTHER READING
Alm, J. (1996), 'What is an optimal tax system?', *National Tax Journal*, **XLIX** (1), 117–133.
Heady, C. (1993), 'Optimal taxation as a guide to tax policy', *Fiscal Studies*, **14** (1), 15–41.
Samuelson, P.A. (1986), 'Theory of optimal taxation', *Journal of Public Economics*, **30** (2), 135–143.

options. The right to buy or sell something at an agreed price at some time in the future.

ordinarily resident. A person who is resident in the country in the normal course of his or her life but may not necessarily be resident for any particular period.

origin principle. The principle that a country in which income originates should be entitled to tax that income. In the case of VAT this would mean that a country would not tax imports and would not refund tax on exports. See also *destination principle*.

outport. In England, all customs ports except that of London.

output. The goods and services produced by an enterprise for sale.

output tax. In a system of *value added tax*, it is the tax charged by the supplier to the customer. See also *input tax*.

outside lag. See *response lag*.

overdue tax. Tax which remains payable after the date on which the tax was due to be paid. Interest is often payable on overdue tax.

overseas. In the UK the terms 'overseas' and 'offshore' may be used rather than 'foreign'. Among other things, it is one way of distinguishing between parts of the British Isles which are not subject to the same tax regimes, for example the Channel Islands and the Isle of Man.

overseas customers. Expenditure on business entertainment is not normally allowable for tax purposes in the UK. An exception is if the entertainment is for overseas customers.

own use. The private use of a business's output by the owner or employees. For the purposes of VAT and income tax this is deemed to be a supply of goods and is therefore subject to tax.

owner occupied homes. A home lived in by the owner. In economic terms this leads to a form of *income in kind*. In this case it is the flow of benefits from living in the house for which a tenant would have to pay rent. In some countries income tax is applied to this benefit less, of course, the costs of maintaining the home. If a loan were used to buy the home, the interest may also be deductible.

P

part disposal. Where part of an asset is disposed of and part retained. The normal treatment for capital gains tax purposes is to apportion the cost of the asset between the two parts.

partial imputation. A version of the *imputation system* in which the corporation tax paid is not always imputed in full to offset shareholders' income tax liability on their dividends.

Partington* v. *Attorney-General. See *literal interpretation of the law.*

passive income. A term used in a similar way to *investment income*, that is to describe income which arrives on its own rather than being the reward to current work. The main examples are dividends, interest and rent.

PAYE. Pay-as-you-earn, the UK system of withholding tax at source and sometimes referred to as Pay-all-you-earn. Introduced in the UK in 1944, it is based on the cumulative principle which works with sufficient accuracy so that it is not necessary to require most British taxpayers to complete a tax return each year. See also *Cumulation.*

payroll tax. A tax on employers' payments of wages, salaries and other forms of remuneration. The tax does not take into account the circumstances of individual employees. As a tax on labour rather than capital it does not help to promote employment. Social security taxation often takes the form of a payroll tax of one sort or another.

penalties. Penalties for non-compliance can take various forms. Some are automatic administrative charges for failure, for example, to submit a tax return on time. Others are discretionary and may be reduced if, for example, the taxpayer co-operates with the revenue authority in an investigation in which the taxpayer is at fault. Other penalties form part of the criminal law of a country. It has been suggested that it might be better to have rewards for compliant behaviour rather than penalties for non-compliance. With an adjustment in tax rates the revenue raised could be the same but tax administration might appear more positive.

Pension. A regular payment made in respect of past service or on retirement. Pension schemes often receive favourable tax treatment, partly to encourage private provision for old age.

FURTHER READING
Eden, S. (1996), 'A history of the taxation of private pensions', *British Tax Review*, 46–70.

PEP. *Personal equity plan.*

Pepper v. Hart [1992] STC 898. A case which provided a precedent for courts to consult parliamentary debates to help interpret legislation. Lord Browne-Wilkinson stated (at p. 923):

> I therefore reach the conclusion, subject to any question of parliamentary privilege, that the exclusionary rule should be relaxed so as to permit reference to parliamentary materials where:
> (a) legislation is ambiguous or obscure, or leads to an absurdity;
> (b) the material relied on consists of one or more statements by a minister or other promoter of the Bill together if necessary, with such other parliamentary material as is necessary to understand such statements and their effect;
> (c) the statements relied upon are clear.
> Further than this I would not at present go.

peppercorn rent. A rent which is only nominal. In earlier times a peppercorn was used to meet the formal requirements of consideration passing in a contract.

perceptibility. The degree to which taxpayers are conscious of their tax liability. It has been held to be an advantage for a tax. For example, John Stuart Mill stated:

> The very reason which makes direct taxation disagreeable, makes it preferable ... If all taxes were direct, taxation would be much more perceived than at present; and there would be a security which now there is not, for economy in the public expenditure.

> *Principles of Political Economy*, bk. V, ch. VI, 1.

Perceptibility was one of the reasons for the introduction of the *community charge*, a form of poll tax, as a means of local taxation in the UK. However, it was too perceptible and abolished in 1993.

perk. An abbreviation of perquisite. See *fringe benefits*.

personal allowance. The amount of income an individual might receive in his or her own right without attracting tax liability. Sometimes known as personal reliefs or exemptions, there may be a single allowance for each individual, a different allowance for married or older people or for children. In some countries, such as the UK, tax allowances for children have been replaced by cash payments. This has the advantage of giving help to those with incomes too low to take full advantage of their personal allowances. It has been suggested that the principle should be extended to the main personal allowance. One such *tax credit* scheme was developed in the early 1970s in the UK.

Personal equity plan (PEP). A scheme operated in the UK and intended to encourage investment in shares. An individual aged 18 or over may invest in shares held by an authorised manager up to a specified limit each year. All income and capital gains arising within the personal equity plan are free of tax. In any tax year a person may also invest in a single company PEP where the investment is limited to the shares of a particular company.

Personal pension plan. An arrangement which enables individuals with eligible earnings to pay contributions into a personal fund which will be used in due course to buy a retirement pension. Within certain limits such contributions attract full tax relief.

personal use property. US term for property owned for personal rather than business use.

petroleum revenue tax (PRT). A UK tax based on the revenue from selling oil and gas from the North Sea less the costs of finding and extracting it.

PFICs. Passive Foreign Investment Company provisions – part of the US Tax Reform Act, 1986.

FURTHER READING
Kaplan, P.T. (1991), 'PFICs', *British Tax Review*, 248–277.

Pigou, A.C. (1877–1959).   Economist making a significant contribution to public finance and particularly remembered for the treatment of external effects. See *Pigovian tax*.

FURTHER READING
Pigou, A.C. (1928), *A Study in Public Finance*, London: Macmillan.

Pigovian tax.   Named after the economist A.C. *Pigou*, it is a tax on an external cost. See *external effect*.

Pitt, William (1759–1806).   Known as 'Pitt the Younger', responsible for the introduction of income tax in 1799.

planning.   See *tax planning*.

plant and machinery.   For tax purposes the definition of plant and machinery relies heavily on the facts of the case. A judgment still cited is that of Lindley LJ in *Yarmouth* v. *France* (1887) 19 QBD 647 at p. 658:

> There is no definition of plant in the Act: but in its ordinary sense, it includes whatever apparatus is used by a businessman for carrying on his business – not his stock-in-trade, which he buys or makes for sale; but all goods and chattels, fixed or movable, live or dead which he keeps for permanent employment in his business.

Plant and machinery form one the most important categories of depreciable assets.

political business cycle.   The theory that governments manipulate public expenditure and taxation in order to win elections. The evidence for the UK suggests that governments do not always use macroeconomic policy for this purpose. One possible reason is that in the UK, unlike some other countries, the timing of general elections is determined by the Prime Minister, who takes account of the prevailing circumstances. It is difficult, therefore, to manipulate the economy in this way when the date of the election need not be fixed until a few weeks in advance. It has been suggested that fixed-term parliaments would lead to greater stability in government policy. However, the outcome might be the opposite. If the date of the election were fixed years in advance it might increase the temptation for governments to try to arrange the economic cycle to fit conveniently with the predetermined political one.

FURTHER READING
Norhaus, W.D. (1975), 'The political business cycle', *Review of Economic Studies*, **2**, 169–190.

poll tax. A lump-sum tax levied on each person, also known as a head or capitation tax. Poll refers to the head of a person or the part of the head on which hair grows, but baldness does not give exemption. Poll taxes can generate considerable opposition. The rising of 1381 arose from a hatred of the poll tax. The Archbishop of Canterbury who, as Chancellor of the realm, represented the government, was beheaded by *Wat Tyler*'s men on Tower Hill and, quite remarkably, the rebels captured London itself. The tax was used by colonial governments in Africa and by the Southern states of the USA after the American Civil War as a method of allocating voting privileges. A more modern manifestation of the poll tax – the UK *community charge*, also generated widespread hostility and had to be abandoned.

FURTHER READING
Gibson, J. (1990), *The Politics and Economics of the Poll Tax: Mrs Thatcher's Downfall*, Warley: EMAS.
Sabine, B. (1992), 'A Stormy Collection – Anno Domini 1381', *British Tax Review*, 395–397.

pollution tax. A tax designed to confront a person or company causing pollution with a sum equivalent to the social costs they are imposing on others. See also *external effect*.

popular tax. Widely thought to be an oxymoron. However, in a debate in the Canadian Parliament in 1917, Sir Thomas White stated that 'In such experience as I have had with taxation – and it has been considerable – there is only one tax that is popular and that is the tax that is on the other fellow'.

post-cessation receipts. Income which arises after a business has ceased and which has not been included in the final accounts.

post-transactions rulings. Tax *rulings* given after a transaction is undertaken.

postwar credits.   Compulsory saving introduced in the UK during the Second World War in order to reduce consumption and release resources for the war effort. The idea came from John Maynard Keynes who considered it to have the additional advantage of stimulating expenditure if there were a postwar slump. Such a scheme has some of the features of a tax and it is perhaps surprising that it has not been used more often.

poverty trap.   The situation where the combined effects of direct taxation and the withdrawal of income-related benefits as income rises means that a person earning more has little or no extra *disposable income*. See also *unemployment trap*.

PPP.   *Personal pension plan*.

practitioners.   See *tax practitioners*.

preceding year basis of assessment.   The arrangement whereby income is charged to tax in any one year on the basis of the preceding year's taxable income. See also *current year basis of assessment*.

preferential tariff.   A *tariff* imposed at lower rates either on the imports from particular countries or on particular goods.

Prest, A.R. (1919–1985).   Economist who contributed to the discussion of many aspects of taxation. He will be remembered by many students for his textbook *Public Finance in Theory and Practice* which was the best in the field for many years.

presumptive tax.   Taxation based on an estimate of a taxpayer's income.

pre-transaction rulings.   Tax *rulings* given before a transaction is carried out.

principal payment.   In a loan repayable in instalments, it is that part of the payments representing the repayment of capital as opposed to the payment of interest.

probate.   The official proving of a will.

probate duty. An early form of *estate duty* introduced in the UK in 1694.

probate value. The value of a deceased person's estate for the purposes of *inheritance tax*.

profit. Revenue minus cost.

FURTHER READING
Pagan, J.C. (1992), 'Measurement of commercial profit for tax purposes', *British Tax Review*, 75–81.

profit and loss account. A financial statement of a firm's income, expenses and profit.

profit-related pay. Pay which is related to a company's profits, usually in addition to normal wages and salaries. It is argued that there are advantages to this arrangement since workers may identify more directly with the commercial success of their firm. There may also be a greater flexibility in difficult times since a reduction in profit-related pay may avoid the need to reduce the number of jobs. In recognition of such possible benefits, tax arrangements have been introduced to encourage the development of profit-related pay.

progressive tax. A tax which takes a higher proportion of higher incomes than it does from lower incomes. A tax may take more in absolute terms from the rich than it does from the poor and still not be progressive if it does not take a bigger proportion of the higher incomes. In technical terms, the definition of a progressive tax is that the *marginal rate of tax* exceeds the *average rate of tax*.

property. *Assets* of individuals or enterprises. Often taken to mean particular types of assets, most commonly land and buildings.

property tax. A tax based on the value of property, though it is often limited to certain types of property such as land and buildings. In some countries it is an important source of *local government finance*. See also *Proposition 13*.

FURTHER READING
Carroll, R.J. and J. Yinger (1994), 'Is the property tax a benefit tax? The case of rental housing', *National Tax Journal*, **XLVII**, (2), 295–316.

proportional tax.   A tax which takes the same proportion of incomes however large or small they are. The term may also be applied to other tax bases such as wealth. In technical terms, the definition of a proportional tax is that the *marginal rate of tax* is equal to the *average rate of tax*.

Proposition 13.   A referendum in California which imposed an upper limit on the taxation on residential property.

FURTHER READING
O'Sullivan, A., T.A. Sexton and S.M Sheffrin (1994), 'Differential Burdens of Proposition 13'. *National Tax Journal*, **XLVII** (4), 721–729.
O'Sullivan, A., T.A. Sexton and S.M Sheffrin (1995), *Property Taxes and Tax Revolts: The Legacy of Proposition 13*, Cambridge: Cambridge University Press.

prostitution.   An activity sometimes advanced as the source of otherwise unexplained income. Nevertheless earnings from prostitution are taxable. It has been suggested that it is a profession, the oldest; and that some inspectors have brought such earnings into tax under Schedule D Case VI – 'furnished lettings'!

provisional collection of taxes.   Legal authority to collect taxes before the proposals have formally been passed as a *Finance Act*.

provisional tax.   The payment of tax in instalments in advance of assessment.

PRP.   *Profit-related pay.*

PRT.   *Petroleum revenue tax.*

psychology.   See *fiscal psychology.*

public choice theory.   An approach to the analysis of public expenditure and taxation which is based on the analysis of the behaviour of politicians and voters.

FURTHER READING
Downs, A. (1957), *An Economic Theory of Democracy*, New York: Harper.
Mueller, D.C. (1979), *Public Choice*, Cambridge: Cambridge University Press.

public finance. The subject area which is devoted to the study of taxation and public expenditure.

FURTHER READING
Musgrave, R.A. (1959), *The Theory of Public Finance*, New York: McGraw-Hill.
Musgrave, R.A. and P.B. (1959), *Public Finance in Theory and Practice*, 5th edn, New York: McGraw-Hill.

public goods. Public goods are a possible source of market failure and thus a justification for government intervention which would usually be paid for by taxation. A pure public good has three economic characteristics. It is 'non-excludable', that is consumers cannot be prevented from consuming it, even if they do not pay for it. Firms cannot therefore normally make a profit from supplying it in a purely market economy. Secondly a public good may be 'non-rival in consumption' – having been produced everyone can consume the public good without displacing anyone else's consumption. Thirdly a public good may be 'non-rejectable', that is having been produced individual consumers cannot refuse to consume it. An example of a public good with all three characteristics is national defence. In practice, different public goods may have one or more of these characteristics and they may be present in different degrees. Others may also have these features in a local area, which has implications for *local government finance*.

purchase tax. In the UK, purchase tax was levied at the wholesale stage of production. It was therefore relatively simple to administer, with between 60 000 and 80 000 collection points, and involved about 1500 civil servants. It was introduced in 1940 and by the late 1950s was levied at three rates of up to 25 per cent. The higher rates were levied on 'luxury' items. Purchase tax was abolished together with *selective employment tax* in 1973 on the introduction of *value added tax*.

PY.   Preceding year. See *preceding year basis of assessment*.

Q

qualifying distribution. In the UK the distribution of dividends or assets which requires the payment of *advance corporation tax*.

questionable payments. Irregular payments made to secure contracts or, in other words, bribes or *secret commissions*.

quick succession relief. A reduction in liability to inheritance tax where a person dies soon after receiving an inheritance which has already been taxed. In the UK the tax levied on the second estate is reduced as follows:

Second death within (years)	Percentage reduction
1	100
2	80
3	60
4	40
5	20

R

Ramsey principle. An important decision reached in *W.T. Ramsey Ltd.* v. *IRC* and *Eilbeck* v. *Rawling* [1981] STC 174. Basically it was held that complicated artificial tax avoidance schemes could be ignored for tax purposes. The essence of the judgment was that courts could look beyond a single transaction to the relevant arrangements as a whole. Lord Wilberforce referred to the *Duke of Westminster* case and said:

> While obliging the court to accept documents or transactions, found to be genuine, as such, it does not compel the court to look at a document or a transaction in blinkers, isolated from any context to which it properly belongs. If it can be seen that a document or transaction was intended to have effect as part of a nexus or series of transactions, or as an ingredient of the wider transaction intended as a whole, there is nothing in the doctrine to prevent it being so regarded: to do so is not to prefer form to substance, or substance to form. It is the task of the court to ascertain the legal nature of any transaction to which it is sought to attach a tax or a tax consequence and if that emerges from a series or combination of transactions, intended to operate as such, it is that series or combination which may be regarded (at p. 180).

See also *Furniss* v. *Dawson*.

Ramsey rules. A piece of economic analysis which suggests that taxes on different goods should have the effect of reducing the demand for them in proportion. There are, however, some qualifications to this analysis. There are also unfortunate implications, the main one of which is that a tax system set up on this basis would bear more heavily on 'necessities' than it would on 'luxuries'.

FURTHER READING
Ramsey, F.P. (1927), 'A contribution to the theory of taxation', *Economic Journal*, **37** (March), 47–61.
Baumol, W.J. and D.F. Bradford (1970), 'Optimal departures from marginal cost pricing', *American Economic Review*, **60**, 265–83.

rate rebates. A subsidy for low income people to assist them paying their *rates*.

rates. A tax on property used to fund local public expenditure. Local authority rates have roots dating back to the Elizabethan Poor Law which accepted public responsibility for the poor and under which resources were found by levying a local rate in each parish. Rates were calculated on the basis of the 'rateable value' of property. Domestic ratepayers were charged at a lower rate than business ratepayers and there were rate rebates for individuals on low incomes. Rates attracted criticism over the years. In particular it was argued that they did not normally take account of individuals' *ability to pay*. Other criticisms came from the local authorities themselves who claimed that rates were not a buoyant source of revenue and that they were too unpopular to raise the increasing amount of revenue required. Rates became increasingly supplemented by grants from central government. Finally, domestic rates were replaced by the *community charge* in Scotland in 1989 and in England and Wales in 1990 and business rates were replaced by the uniform *business rate*. The community charge did not prove to be a success and was replaced by the *council tax* in 1993.

realisations basis. Tax is calculated with reference to the date an asset is sold. This is the usual basis for *capital gains tax*. It is administratively simpler than taxing capital gains as they accrue but it can leave taxpayers '*locked-in*' to particular assets. See also *accruals basis*.

real property tax. A tax on land and buildings.

recognition lag. The time taken for the government to recognise that there is a need to adjust *fiscal policy*. This can occur for a number of reasons. One is that there are delays before economic statistics can be collected, analysed and published. Another important one is that even when such statistics begin to indicate that something might be happening in the economy, it can be difficult to decide whether this might be the start of a recession or a temporary downturn in economic activity. See also *implementation lag* and *response lag*.

redistribution. It has been argued that one of the functions of government is to redistribute spending power in society through taxation and public expenditure. See *distribution function*.

reform. See *tax reform*.

regressive tax. A tax which takes a higher proportion of low incomes than it does from higher incomes. A tax may still be regressive even if it takes more from those on higher incomes if it takes a lower proportion of those incomes. In technical terms, the definition of a regressive tax is that the *marginal rate of tax* is less than the *average rate of tax*.

rent. See *economic rent*.

replacement ratio. The ratio of social security payments made while unemployed to the net income received while working. High replacement ratios are likely to generate disincentive effects to work. See *poverty trap* and *unemployment trap*.

research and development. A form of investment which has generated some discussion about how far it should attract tax relief.

FURTHER READING
Griffith, R. (1995), D. Sandler and J. Van Reenen, 'Tax incentives for R & D', *Fiscal Studies*, **16** (2), 21–44.

response lag. The time taken for the economy to adjust to a change in *fiscal policy*. It is also sometimes known as the *outside lag*.

retained earnings. Profit retained within an incorporated enterprise rather than distributed to shareholders. It may be subject to some form of *corporate taxation*.

returns. A declaration of income and other information required by the tax authorities for the purposes of assessing the taxpayer and sometimes to gather information about the taxable circumstances of other parties. One of the earliest returns was given in an Act (39 Geo 3, c. 22) following the introduction of income tax in the UK in 1799. It was a straightforward self-assessment return (see Figure R.1).

revenue sharing. The transfer of funds from central to local government, or from federal to state governments. This arises since it is not always easy for the lower levels of government to raise sufficient revenue for their needs. Also it is usual for some parts of a country to be more prosperous than other parts, and revenue sharing permits a certain amount of redistribution.

I   do declare that I am willing to pay the sum
of   for my contribution for one year, from the fifth day of April
        until the fifth day of April   in pursuance of an Act passed
in the thirty-ninth year of the reign of His present Majesty intituled ...
[the full name of the Act was entered here] and of another Act for
amending the said Act; and I do declare that the said sum of   is
not less than one tenth part of my income, estimated according to the
directions and rules prescribed by the said Acts, to the best of my
knowledge and belief. Dated this day of
                              Signed

Figure R.1   The original income tax return

revenue support grant.   In the UK a payment from central taxation
revenues to help support local authority services.

reverse income tax.   See *negative income tax.*

Ricardo, David (1772–1823).   Highly influential nineteenth century
economist who presented an early analysis of the effects of taxation.

FURTHER READING
Ricardo, D. (1817), *On the Principles of Political Economy and Taxation*, London: J.
   Murray.

ring fence.   The isolation for tax purposes of a group of activities
from other activities. This may be to ensure that only costs incurred
within the ring fence may be set against the revenues arising from the
activities within the ring fence. For example, such a provision has been
used by the UK to prevent oil companies from using tax losses and
reliefs from activities on the mainland and the rest of the world to
reduce their taxable profits from North Sea oilfields.

risk taking.   Economic enterprise usually involves commercial risk
and therefore it is important to know how a tax system affects the
willingness of entrepreneurs to take risks. If profits are taxed but no
allowances are made for losses when they occur, this will reduce the
expected return from undertaking commercial ventures. In other words,
the government will share in the gains when a business is successful,

but in more difficult times the owners are left with the entire losses. It is therefore usual for businesses to be able to claim relief for losses made in the normal course of their activities.

FURTHER READING
James, S. and C. Nobes (1996), *The Economics of Taxation*, 5th edn., London: Prentice Hall.
Kaplow, L. (1994), 'Taxation and risk taking: A general equilibrium perspective', *National Tax Journal*, **XLVII** (4), 789–798.

rolled up interest.   Interest which becomes payable only when a bond matures. There may be a tax advantage if such a payment were accepted by the revenue authorities as a capital gain rather than income.

roll-over relief.   A relief sometimes available for the purposes of the taxation of *capital gains*. When an enterprise sells an asset any capital gain may be deductible against the cost of a replacement asset.

roof tax.   A domestic property tax.

Rooker–Wise Amendment.   An amendment to the UK tax legislation in 1975 requiring that personal allowances be increased in line with the increase in retail prices unless Parliament specified otherwise.

Rossminster.   The name of a bank which was associated with the tax *avoidance* industry. The Inland Revenue carried out a well-publicised series of raids starting at 7 a.m. on 13 July 1979 which did much to stop certain practices.

FURTHER READING
Tutt, N. (1985), *The Tax Raiders: The Rossminster Affair*, London: Financial Training Publishers.

royal taxation.   The tax treatment of royal families – a topic which arouses considerable interest from time to time.

FURTHER READING
Bartlett, R.T. (1983), 'Taxation and the Royal Family', *British Tax Review*, 99–112 and 138–157.
Pearce-Crump, D. (1994), 'Royal taxation', *British Tax Review*, 635–646.

royalty.   In taxation, a royalty is a tax paid to a government for the right to extract minerals.

Ruding Committee.   Set up by the European Commission to investigate the case for company tax harmonisation in the European Union.

FURTHER READING
Gammie, M. (1992), 'The harmonisation of corporate income taxes in Europe: The Ruding Committee Report', *Fiscal Studies*, **13** (2), 108–121.
Ruding Committee (1992), *Conclusions and Recommendations of the Committee of Independent Experts on Company Taxation*, Luxembourg: Commission of the European Communities.

The 'Rule'.   Schedule E, Rule 9, ITA 1918, dealing with *employment expenses*. See also *wholly, exclusively and necessarily*.

rulings.   Official interpretations of legislative provisions. In many tax systems, taxpayers ask how the law might be applied in particular circumstances. Usually tax rulings are given by revenue authorities but there are exceptions. For example, in Sweden tax rulings are issued by an independent body.

FURTHER READING
James, S. and I. Wallschutzky (1995), 'The design of an appropriate system of tax rulings, *Revenue Law Journal*, **5** (2), 175–196.
Sandler, D. (1994), *A Request for Rulings*, London: Institute of Taxation/Institute for Fiscal Studies.

S

sacrifice approach. An analysis of the ability to pay approach. It assumes that income and *utility* are correlated. It also supposes that everyone has the same utility function which slopes downwards – in other words the more money a person has, the less he or she values each extra unit. It then suggests three possibilities – that taxpayers should make an equal *sacrifice* of utility, an *equi-proportional sacrifice* or a *least aggregate sacrifice*. Among the difficulties with this approach is that it is very unlikely that everyone has the same utility function or even that it always slopes downwards.

sales taxes. Taxes on goods and services at the point of sale.

FURTHER READING
Fox, W.F. (ed.) (1992), *Sales Taxation: Critical Issues in Policy and Administration*, Westport: Praeger.

savings. Income not spent on consumption. Saving is often held to be desirable for a number of reasons. It releases resources for investment and it provides individuals with economic security. As a result there are frequently tax advantages to saving.

FURTHER READING
Boadway, R. and D. Wildasin (1994), 'Taxation and savings: A survey', *Fiscal Studies*, **15** (3), 19–63.

Schedules and the schedular system. Taxation can be assessed and collected under different schedules. In the UK, the original system of income tax introduced in 1799 proved unpopular, partly because a total return of income had been required and this was considered an infringement of privacy. From 1803, income tax was assessed under five schedules – A, B, C, D and E. Taxpayers then declared their income received separately under each schedule so that no official needed to know their total income. In fact returns of total income were not required again until the introduction of supertax in 1909. Although there have been some changes in the scope of the schedules and a new Schedule F was introduced in 1965 the basic structure still resembles the 1803 provisions. The schedules are:

Schedule A: Income from land and buildings.
Schedule B: Income from commercial woodlands. This schedule
was abolished from April 1988.
Schedule C: Interest from government securities.
Schedule D: Income from self-employment and other business and
property income.
Schedule E: Income from employment.
Schedule F: Distributions subject to higher rate tax.

FURTHER READING
Sheridan, D. (1991), 'Sources of income and Schedule E', *British Tax Review*, 214–223.

scientific tariff. A *tariff* imposed to achieve a particular policy objective and levied at a rate calculated to minimise the economic cost to society. See also *optimal tariff*.

scutage. From the Latin *scutum*, meaning shield, scutage was money paid to the king instead of military service. King John substantially increased the revenues from scutage with the result that Clause 16 of the *Magna Carta* specifically restricted the imposition of scutage.

SDRT. Stamp duty reserve tax.

secret commission. An illegal payment or bribe made to secure a contract or receive some service.

seigniorage. The gain made by a government in creating money. See *inflation tax*.

selective employment tax (SET). A tax on payrolls which was then refunded to manufacturing industry, sometimes with a bonus. The reason for its introduction was that the existing *purchase tax* was thought to discriminate against goods rather than services. SET was therefore introduced to encourage labour to move towards manufacturing which, in some circles, was thought to be more productive than services. It was very unpopular with small traders and the acronym SET was sometimes expanded as 'silliest ever tax', though the competition for that distinction in tax history is very tough. It was eventually abolished along with purchase tax in 1973 on the introduction of *value added tax*.

FURTHER READING
Reddaway, W.B. (1973), *Effects of Selective Employment Tax: Final Report*, Cambridge University Press.

self-assessment. A system of taxation where the taxpayer rather than the revenue service is primarily responsible for calculating tax liability and ensuring that payment is made promptly.

FURTHER READING
James, S. (1995), *Self-Assessment and the UK Tax System*, London: Research Board of the Institute of Chartered Accountants in England and Wales.

self-employment. The definition of self-employment as opposed to employment varies between tax jurisdictions and the two categories are sometimes treated differently for tax purposes. See also *employment*.

FURTHER READING
Freedman, J. and E. Chamberlain (1997), 'Horizontal equity and the taxation of employed and self-employed workers', *Fiscal Studies*, **18** (1), 87–118.

settlements. An arrangement whereby property is held under a trust.

FURTHER READING
Stopforth, D. (1991), 'The first attack on settlements used for income tax avoidance', *British Tax Review*, 86–103.

shadow economy. Another term for the *black economy*.

sham. A document or transaction which is not what it professes to be. In *Snook* v. *London & West Riding Investments Ltd* [1967] 2QB 786 at p. 802, Diplock L.J. said that a sham:

> means acts done or documents executed by the parties to the 'sham' which are intended by them to give to third parties or to the court the appearance of creating between the parties legal rights and obligations different from the actual legal rights and obligations (if any) which the parties intend to create.

shifting of taxes. The way in which the tax burden is shifted around the economy through changes in prices and other economic variables. See *incidence of taxation*.

Shoup Mission. A mission headed by Carl S. Shoup, an American expert in Public Finance, which reviewed the Japanese tax system and administration following the end of the Second World War. It produced recommendations which were incorporated in the tax reforms of 1950. The overall tax reform saw direct taxation, particularly income tax and corporation tax, as the central part of the tax system. Also the *blue return system* was developed in order to reform the process of tax administration.

SI.   Statutory instrument.

simplicity.   A much sort after virtue in tax administration but not one easily achieved. One approach has been to simplify the language but that is difficult if the system itself remains complex. One relevant example was reported by Sir Alexander Johnston. The Board of Inland Revenue had sent Lloyd George, who was then Chancellor of the Exchequer, a paper about estate duty liability on settled property:

> Mr Lloyd George rejected this paper and demanded an explanation in words of one syllable. The Board sent a new paper – in words of one syllable; but the subject matter remained as complicated as before, and the monosyllables made it rather harder to understand.

However more recent work in this area has been done by the Inland Revenue and the Tax Law Review Committee. See also *comprehensibility* and *fiscal fog*.

FURTHER READING
Cooper, G.S. (1993), 'Themes and issues in tax simplification', *Australian Tax Forum*, **10** (4), 417–460.
Inland Revenue (1995), *The Path to Tax Simplification*, London: HMSO.
Sir Alexander Johnston (1965), *The Inland Revenue*, London: Allen & Unwin, p. 56.
Tax Law Review Committee (1996), *Final Report on Tax Legislation*, London: Institute for Fiscal Studies.

single tax movement.   A campaign led by Henry George in the USA for all existing taxes to be replaced by a single tax on land.

FURTHER READING
George, H. (1883), *Progress and Poverty*, Kegan Paul, London: Trench & Co.

sin taxes.   Taxes on alcohol, tobacco and other activities which the authorities may consider not to be good for us.

small business. There are many definitions of a small business but they are usually linked to turnover, profits or employees. It has been argued that small businesses should be taxed more lightly than larger businesses. See also *small companies rate*.

FURTHER READING
Holz-Eakin, D. (1995), 'Should small businesses be tax-favoured?', *National Tax Journal*, **XLVIII** (3), 387–395.

small companies rate. A lower rate of *corporation tax*, though it applies to companies with smaller profits rather than small companies. There is a *tapering relief* to ease the transition to the full rate of corporation tax which is incurred when profits rise.

social security contributions. A form of tax which is usually linked with welfare payments. In the UK they take the form of *National Insurance contributions*.

soft loan. A loan with a concessionary interest rate set at a level below interest rates generally.

sole trader. An unincorporated business which is owned by a single person, though it may have any number of employees.

Somerset House. Occupied by the Inland Revenue and its predecessors since 1785 – originally by the Commissioners of Taxes and the Stamp Office. Located in the Strand, London, it was first occupied by the Lord Protector Somerset.

Special Commissioners. See *Commissioners of Income Tax*.

specific tax. A tax imposed per unit of output of a good rather than on value.

spendings tax. See *expenditure tax*.

spite effect. The response by taxpayers of reducing their tax liability even if the result is costly to them, for example by working less. This might happen because of anger aroused by the tax, a desire for revenge against the government or because taxpayers might hope to persuade the government to reduce the tax. If there is a spite effect it is more likely to be associated with visible taxes, such as income tax, than with more hidden taxes

FURTHER READING
Musgrave, R.A. (1959), *The Theory of Public Finance*, New York: McGraw-Hill.

split-rate system.   A form of corporate taxation in which a lower rate of tax is applied to distributed profits than the rate applying to retained profits. The aim is to reduce or remove the *double taxation of dividends*. See also *classical system* and *imputation system*.

Smith, Adam (1723–1790).   Widely considered to be the founder of modern political economy, Smith's famous book *The Wealth of Nations* included a whole section on 'the revenue of the Sovereign or Commonwealth'. His canons or principles of taxation are still quoted as a highly perceptive introduction to the subject. See *canons of taxation*.

FURTHER READING
Smith, A. (1776), *An Inquiry into the Nature and Causes of the Wealth of Nations*, London: W. Strahan and T. Cadell.

s(ss).   section or sections of an Act of Parliament.

SSAP.   Statement of standard accounting practice.

stabilisation function.   One of the economic functions of government though its role in this context has been the subject of considerable debate. Essentially it is the use of fiscal and monetary policy to stabilise fluctuations in economic activity. See also *allocative function* and *distribution function*.

stamp duty.   First introduced in 1694, stamp duty is a tax on certain transactions and evidence of payment is provided by a stamp on the relevant legal document.

FURTHER READING
Jamieson, C. (1991), 'Stamp duties in the European Community: Harmonisation by abolition?', *British Tax Review*, 318–323.
Nock, R S (1994), 'Leases and agreements for lease and the new stamp duty regime', *British Tax Review*, 436–454.

standard deductions.   A specified tax deduction from income in respect of expenses without reference to the actual amount spent.

STC. Simon's tax cases.

stock appreciation relief. A tax relief introduced in the UK in 1973 and repealed in 1984. It was designed to relieve the taxation on unrealised gains on inventories during inflation.

strategic tax planning. An overall strategy to reduce tax liability.

structured settlements. The payment of damages for personal injury or death 'structured' over a period of time to take account of an individual's needs. For the purposes of taxation, such payments may be considered instalments of a capital payment rather than income.

FURTHER READING
Lewis, R. (1994), 'The taxation of structured settlements', *British Tax Review*, 19–31.

submit. UK term for the supply of a tax return to the tax authorities. Sometimes taxpayers have 'furnished' the tax office with their returns. In the US taxpayers file their returns and in Australia they lodge them.

subsidy. This has been defined as a negative tax – a payment from public funds rather than a contribution. Economic analysis of the sort used to analyse taxation is also useful in analysing subsidies.

substitution effect. When the price of a good or service changes there are two reasons why the amount demanded might change – the substitution effect and the *income effect*. The substitution effect describes the shift to or from substitute products as a result of the relative price change. For example, if the price of beer rises, some demand might be transferred to other alcoholic beverages or other items of expenditure. Substitution and income effects are used in the analysis of taxation. For instance, in the analysis of income tax, the substitution effect is associated with changes in the *marginal rate of tax*. If the marginal rate of taxation changes it affects the trade-off between work and leisure and, as a result, individuals may wish to adjust the amount or quality of the work they do. The income effect is associated with the *average rate of tax* which affects the real income or spending power of individuals.

succession tax. See *accessions tax*.

supply-side economics. A school of economic thought based mainly in the USA which was concerned with, among other things, the possible disincentive effects of taxation on the willingness of producers to supply goods and services. One of its most prominent members was Arther Laffer who became particularly well known for his *Laffer curve*.

FURTHER READING
Minford, P. (1991), *The Supply Side Revolution in Britain*, Aldershot: Edward Elgar.

surveyor of taxes. Predecessor of inspectors of taxes and first appears in the Taxing Act of 1656. Sir Josiah Stamp, a former surveyor, observed that 'Monarch of all I inspect is not as impressive as Monarch of all I survey' (quoted in B. Sabine, (1966) *A History of Income Tax*, Allen & Unwin, p. 171).

T

TA. Income and Corporation Taxes Act.

taille. French tax established in the late fourteenth century on each person or household.

take-home pay. Income from employment less tax and National Insurance contributions. A similar concept to *disposable income.*

tallage. Originally a tax levied by Norman monarchs but the word was later used to describe various levies or duties.

tallies. Notched sticks used as receipts for tax or sums paid out.

tangible assets. Physical *assets* such as plant and machinery and stocks. See also *intangible assets.*

tapering relief. A concession sometimes allowed, for example in the UK corporation tax, to ease the transition between a reduced rate of tax and the full rate of tax. Its effect is to withdraw the benefit of the reduced rate gradually as profit rises.

tariff. A tax levied on imports and (sometimes) exports. The term was originally used to describe an official list of *customs duties* imposed on imports and exports. The effect of a tariff on imports is to increase prices in the importing country. This benefits domestic producers but at the expense of domestic consumers. There have been many arguments for tariffs. These include protection from 'dumping' (see *anti-dumping duty*), the *infant industry argument*, to promote a country's self-sufficiency in a product and the *optimal tariff* argument. Such arguments are often unconvincing, particularly as tariffs provide a barrier to trade and a consequent loss of economic prosperity. See, for example, *Hawley-Smoot tariff.*

FURTHER READING
Ratner, S. (1972), *The Tariff in American History*, New York: Van Nostrand.

tariff escalation. The imposition of higher tariffs as the amount of processing of a product increases.

tariff factory. Manufacturing capacity located in a country only to avoid that country's *tariffs* on imported goods.

tariff structure. The overall arrangement of a country's tariffs, which may vary on different goods and on imports from different countries.

tax. A compulsory levy made by public authorities for which nothing is received *directly* in return. There are many varieties of taxation and there are very few items which have not escaped taxation at one time or another. Figure T.1 gives an indication of the different varieties of possible taxes. One distinction is between *direct* and *indirect* taxes. See also *classification of taxes*.

tax abatement. Tax refund because the original charge was too high.

taxable capacity. The amount of tax individuals and organisations can pay.

taxable income. Gross income less allowances and allowable expenses.

taxable person. A person who is required to be registered for the purposes of *value added tax*.

taxable transaction. An economic event which is, potentially at least, liable to taxation.

tax amnesty. See *amnesty*.

tax arbitrage. In normal usage arbitrage means buying in one market and selling at a higher price in another market. Tax arbitrage is where such activity is a result of the tax system. For instance, in some circumstances it may be profitable to borrow money, deduct the interest payable from taxable income, and invest the money elsewhere.

taxator. A person who assesses or levies a tax.

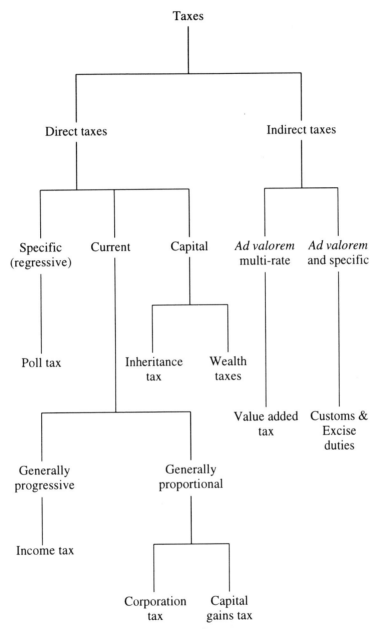

Figure T.1   Different forms of taxation

Source: James, S. and C. Nobes (1996), *The Economics of Taxation*, 5th edn., London: Prentice Hall.

tax avoidance.   See *avoidance*.

tax bankruptcies.   The situation where the tax authority is the only creditor of a bankrupt's estate.

tax base.   That which is liable to taxation, for example, income, wealth or expenditure.

tax bite.   The amount of tax a person has to pay.

tax breaks.   US term for tax concessions.

tax buoyancy.   See *buoyancy*.

tax buoyancy ratio.   There are several definitions, for instance the relationship between the percentage increase in tax revenue and the percentage increase in gross domestic product.

tax burden.   The proportion of a country's income or product which is taken in taxation. To some extent the proportion can be manipulated by using different measures of national income or product. For example, it may be expressed as a percentage of gross national product (GNP), net national product (NNP), gross domestic product (GDP) or net domestic product (NDP) and any of these may be calculated at market prices or at factor cost. See also *excess burden* of taxation.

tax capitalisation.   See *capitalisation*.

tax code.   (1) A number used to determine tax free pay in the *PAYE* scheme. (2) In some countries the whole body of the tax law.

tax competition.   The competition between different tax jurisdictions by using tax concessions to encourage businesses and individuals to locate in their areas.

FURTHER READING
Coates, D. (1993), 'Tax competition among jurisdictions with public and private employ ment', *National Tax Journal*, **XLVI** (2), 177–189.

tax co-ordination.   The attempt to achieve consistent tax regimes across countries. See also *harmonisation*.

FURTHER READING
Keen, M. (1993), 'The welfare economics of tax co-ordination in the European Community', *Fiscal Studies*, **14** (2), 15–36.

tax credit.   (1) A credit against tax. For example, in the UK corporation tax system, company dividends to shareholders are accompanied by a tax credit which is set against shareholders' liability to income tax. (2) A tax credit system is a form of *negative income tax*. Specific proposals for a tax credit scheme were developed by the UK government in the early 1970s. The principle was that if a person's income was insufficient to take full advantage of their *personal allowances*, the difference would be paid out as a cash subsidy. The proposals excluded the self-employed and some other groups and were feasible. However the general election of 1974 brought in a new government and the proposals were not implemented.

tax disc.   A circular certificate denoting the payment of motor *vehicle excise duty* displayed in the window of a motor vehicle.

tax dodger.   A person who engages in tax *avoidance* or tax *evasion*.

tax dollar.   Money paid as tax.

tax eater.   A person who is supported by public expenditure.

tax effort.   The extent to which a revenue authority collects the full legal liability of tax due.

tax elasticity.   The change in the amount of tax revenue raised as the tax base increases. For example, in the case of income, it would be the increase in income tax as incomes rose.

tax equivalent yield.   The yield on a tax-free bond calculated as if the interest were taxable.

taxer.   A person who determines the amount of tax due.

tax erosion.   The extent to which the tax base is reduced by allowances and exemptions. See also *tax expenditure*.

tax evader.   A person who engages in tax *evasion.*

tax-exempt bonds.   Public sector debt paying tax-free interest.

FURTHER READING
Zimmerman, D. (1989), 'Tax-exempt bonds: A sacred cow that gave (some) milk', *National Tax Journal*, **XLII** (3), 283–292.

tax exile.   A person who lives in a foreign country in order to avoid tax.

tax expenditure.   A fiscal advantage associated with a particular activity, or on a group of individuals, by reducing tax liability rather than a direct cash subsidy. The term was coined by Stanley S. Surrey in 1967 while Assistant Secretary for Tax Policy in the US Treasury Department. His description was that tax expenditures are those provisions:

> containing special exemptions, exclusions, and other tax benefits [which] were really methods of providing governmental financial assistance. These special provisions were not part of the structure required for the income tax itself, but were instead government expenditures made through the tax system
>
> (Surrey (1973), p. vii).

Whatever advantages there may be in granting government concessions in this way, there are also significant disadvantages. It might be argued that tax expenditures are relatively 'hidden' and subject to less scrutiny and review than are direct expenditures. They might well therefore continue in force even after the original case for them has diminished, or even disappeared. The value of tax expenditures is different for different individuals, depending on their marginal tax rate and, of course, for non-taxpayers they are worth nothing at all. There may be a lack of co-ordination and anomalies in respect of the regular public expenditure budget. Finally they also complicate the tax system and are often used for the purposes of tax *avoidance* in ways which were never originally intended.

FURTHER READING
Surrey, S.S. (1973), *Pathways to Tax Reform*, Cambridge, MA: Harvard University Press.
Davie, B.F. (1994), 'Tax expenditures in the federal excise tax system, *National Tax Journal*, **XLVII** (1), 39–62.

Table T.1   *Examples of estimated tax expenditures in the UK in 1996/97*

Income tax	£ million
Occupational pension schemes	8000
Married couple's allowance	2800
Mortgage interest relief	2400
Contributions to personal pensions	2200
Profit-related pay	1500
Redundancy payments	1300
Age-related allowances	1000
British government securities owned overseas	700
Child benefit	700
Personal equity plans	600
Incapacity benefit	500
Tax exempt special savings account interest	350
Additional allowance for one-parent family	220
Approved savings – related share option schemes	200
Life assurance premiums (contracts before March 1984)	150
Private medical assurance premiums for the over 60s	120
Approved profit-sharing schemes	100
Approved discretionary share option scheme	80
Capital gains tax	
Disposal of a person's only or main residence	450
Retirement relief	100

Source: *Inland Revenue Statistics* (1996), HMSO.

tax farming.   Privatised tax collection and perhaps assessment also. It is an old system whereby the government sells to private tax collectors the right to collect taxes.

taxflation.   US term which describes the increase in income tax payable as inflation pushes taxpayers into higher tax brackets. See also *bracket creep*.

tax foreclosure.   The seizure by public authorities of property for non-payment of taxes.

tax-free shops.   Shops which may sell goods free of taxation. These are most usually found at ports and airports where passengers can purchase duty-free goods. Such products are not necessarily the bargains they seem. Economic analysis, in addition to casual observation, suggests that the prices may not be reduced by the full amount of the tax.

tax-free threshold.   The amount of income a taxpayer may receive before becoming liable to taxation.

tax gap.   The difference between actual tax revenue and that which would be received if there were 100 per cent compliance on the part of taxpayers. See also *compliance*.

tax gatherer.   A person who collects tax.

tax handles.   Parts of an economic system to which taxes can be attached. In primarily non-market economies there are relatively few tax handles which increases the difficulties of raising taxation.

tax harmonisation.   See *harmonisation*.

tax havens.   Countries or areas where tax rates are substantially lower than those to which a taxpayer would be subject elsewhere.

tax holiday.   A period in which tax is reduced or relieved altogether. Tax holidays are used to encourage businesses to establish themselves in a particular jurisdiction or locality.

tax incidence.   See *incidence of taxation*.

taxing-master.   An officer of a court of law who reviews disputes over lawyers' bills.

tax invoice.   An invoice relating to the supply of goods subject to *value added tax*.

tax literacy.   The ability to complete a tax return properly.

tax loophole.   A feature of the tax system which allows taxpayers to reduce their liability.

tax loss. A loss determined for the purposes of calculating taxable income. There are usually limitations on what may be claimed as a tax loss.

tax legislation. Tax legislation consists of primary legislation which are acts or laws and secondary legislation which may consist of regulations and decisions. Tax legislation is also supplemented by case law.

taxman. An officer of a revenue authority.

tax mix. The relevant importance of different taxes in providing a country's tax revenue. For instance, some countries rely more on *direct taxes* than on *indirect taxes*.

tax neutrality. See *neutrality*.

taxpayer. A person who pays taxes or is liable to pay taxes. It also includes individuals who have died, though there is a time limit on any action which may be taken after death, and enterprises which no longer exist.

Taxpayer Compliance Measurement Programme (TCMP). A system used in the US which is designed to evaluate taxpayer compliance through audits. The results of these audits are used to develop the formula which is used to select taxpayers' returns for audit by identifying features which increase the likelihood that a particular return is unsatisfactory.

taxpayers' charter. Written document specifying rights, obligations and so on in respect of taxation. The Taxpayer's Charter issued by the Inland Revenue states:

You are entitled to expect the Inland Revenue

To be fair
- By settling your tax affairs impartially
- By expecting you to pay only what is due under the law
- By treating everyone with equal fairness

To help you
- To get your tax affairs right

- To understand your rights and obligations
- By providing clear leaflets and forms
- By giving you information at our enquiry offices
- By being courteous at all times

To provide an efficient service
- By settling your tax affairs promptly and accurately
- By keeping your private affairs strictly confidential
- By using the information you give us only as allowed by the law
- By keeping to a minimum your costs of complying with the law
- By keeping our costs down

To be accountable for what we do
- By setting standards for ourselves and publishing how well we live up to them

If you are not satisfied
- We will tell you exactly how to complain
- You can ask for your tax affairs to be looked at again
- You can appeal to an independent tribunal
- Your MP can refer your complaint to the Ombudsman

In return, we need you
- To be honest
- To give us accurate information
- To pay your tax on time

tax planning. The arrangement of the financial affairs of an individual or a business to reduce tax liability insofar as this is compatible with other objectives. Sensible tax planning does not aim to minimise tax liability regardless of other costs incurred and opportunities foregone.

tax point. The date on which any particular transaction becomes chargeable to *value added tax.*

tax policy. William E. Simon, a former Secretary to the US Treasury once said that 'The nation should have a tax system which looks like someone designed it on purpose'. Government policy regarding the tax system frequently comes in for criticism, mainly because it is difficult to meet multiple objectives, particularly in a changing economic and social environment. Ideally tax policy should take account of the requirements of economic efficiency and incentives, equity considerations, macroeconomic policy and existing administrative arrangements.

FURTHER READING
Messere, K. (1993), *Tax Policy in OECD Countries: Choices and Conflicts*, Amsterdam: IBFD Publications.

tax practitioners. Agents who assist individuals and organisations with their tax affairs. In the UK it includes members of the *Chartered Institute of Taxation*, and appropriately qualified accountants and lawyers.

FURTHER READING
Christian, C.W., S. Gupta and S. Lon (1993), 'Determinants of tax preparer usage: Evidence from panel data', *National Tax Journal*, **XLVI** (4), 487–503.

tax raids. The entry and inspection of taxpayers' premises. Some of the most dramatic include the *Rossminster* raids.

tax rate. The extent to which a tax is imposed on the tax base. See also *average rate of tax* and *marginal rate of tax*.

tax rebate. A refund of overpaid tax to a taxpayer.

tax reform. Successful tax reform is more difficult to achieve than seems to be widely perceived. R.M. Bird and O. Oldman in *Taxation in Developing Countries* (4th edn., 1990, p. 3) put it as follows:

> The best approach to reforming taxes ... is one that takes into account taxation theory, empirical evidence, and political and administrative realities and blends them with a good dose of local knowledge and a sound appraisal of the current macroeconomic and international situation to produce a feasible set of proposals sufficiently attractive to be implemented and sufficiently robust to withstand changing times, within reason, and still produce beneficial results.

In the UK, the Inland Revenue uses a range of considerations in evaluating proposals, and a list of the main ones appeared in the 1986 Public Expenditure White Paper (HM Treasury, 1986, vol. 2, p. 314). They were:

i)   the cost or yield to the Exchequer and the distribution of gainers and losers among different categories of taxpayer;
ii) the economic effects of the proposals and any behavioural changes they would be likely to induce;
iii) the consistency of the proposals with the general thrust of the Government's tax policy, and its broader economic, financial and social policies;

iv)   the implications for other parts of the tax system, for the social
       security system, or for other proposals which ministers may be con-
       sidering;
v)   the likely effect on the perceived fairness and general acceptability
       of the tax system;
vi)   the effect of the proposals in increasing or reducing the complexity
       of the tax system;
vii)   the administrative implications, including effects of public expendi-
       ture and the use of public service manpower;
viii) the compliance burden on employers, businesses and other taxpayers;
ix)   any views bearing on the proposals expressed in Parliament, or by
       representative bodies or by individual taxpayers;
x)   any relevant international obligations arising from, for example
       double taxation agreements or European Community obligations.

See also *forcefield analysis.*

FURTHER READING
Slemrod, J. and J. Bakija (1996), *Taxing Ourselves: A Citizen's Guide to the Great
    Debate over Tax Reform*, Cambridge: MIT Press.

tax relief.   A concession in respect of tax which would otherwise be
payable.

tax return.   See *returns.*

tax roll.   US term for the record of taxpayers and taxable property
maintained by cities and towns.

tax shelter.   An arrangement of business affairs in order to reduce tax
liability.

tax shifting.   The way in which the burden of taxation can be shifted
around an economic system. See *incidence of taxation.*

tax tables.   Tables issued by the Inland Revenue to enable employers
to calculate the correct amount of tax to withhold under the UK *PAYE*
system.

tax taker.   Tax collector.

tax threshold.   The level of the tax base at which tax is levied. For
example, normally individuals can receive a certain amount of income

before becoming liable to income tax. There may also be higher thresholds for higher rates of tax. It is also known as the tax-free threshold.

tax training. There has been much discussion about the appropriate tax training and education of tax officials and tax practitioners. It is becoming more widely recognised that there is a case for supplementing initial technical training and there are increasing developments in terms of university education in taxation and continuing professional development.

FURTHER READING
James, S. and C. Evans (1996), 'A comparison of the education and training of taxation professionals and officials in the United Kingdom and Australia', *British Tax Review*, 438–450.

tax unit. The tax unit may consist of individuals (see *individual basis of taxation*) or a family (see *aggregation basis of taxation*).

tax wedge. The difference between the price paid by consumers and that received by suppliers as a result of the imposition of a tax. The term is also used to refer to the *excess burden* of taxation.

tax year. See *year*.

TCMP. *Taxpayer Compliance Measurement Programme.*

'ten forty'. See *1040*.

TESSA. Tax-exempt special savings account.

theft. Within limits, petty theft from a business by subordinates may be deductible for tax purposes. In *Curtis v. J & G Oldfield* [1925] 9 TC 319 at p. 330, Rowlatt J. said:

> if you have a business ... in the course of which you have to employ subordinates, and owing to the negligence or the dishonesty of the subordinates some of the receipts of the business do not find their way into the till, or some of the bills are not collected at all, or something of that sort, that may be an expense connected with and arising out of the trade in the most complete sense of the word.

thin capitalisation.   The practice of financing foreign operations through debt rather than equity where this can shift tax liability from high tax countries to low tax countries.

FURTHER READING
Sommerhalder, R.A. (1996), 'Approaches to thin capitalisation', *European Taxation*, **36** (3), 82–95.

threshold effect.   An increase in the amount of taxation a population is willing to pay to meet some crisis such as war. Once the previous 'threshold' of acceptable taxation has been exceeded, it has been argued, taxpayers remain willing to pay higher taxes even when the crisis has passed. See *displacement effect*.

Tiebout model.   A model of local government in which individuals move between local government jurisdictions to those areas which are more compatible with their preferences regarding local public spending and taxation.

FURTHER READING
Tiebout, C.M. (1956), 'A pure theory of local government expenditures', *Journal of Political Economy*, **64** (3), 416–424.

tight fiscal policy.   A policy in which taxes are relatively high or public expenditure relatively restricted or both.

time limits.   The period within which certain actions have to be taken if they are to be valid. For example, in the UK an assessment or additional assessment cannot be made after six years from the end of the relevant tax year except in cases of fraud or negligent conduct.

tithe.   One of the oldest forms of taxation, consisting of a fixed proportion, usually a tenth, of agricultural produce, earnings and so on.

TMA.   Taxes Management Act 1970.

TNCs.   Transnational corporations.

tobacco taxation.   Like alcohol, tobacco has been a favourite target for taxation because its price elasticity of demand is thought to be low and in more recent years because of possible harmful effects of tobacco consumption.

FURTHER READING

Gravelle, J. and D. Zimmerman (1994), 'Cigarette taxes to fund health care reform', *National Tax Journal*, **XLVII** (3), 575–590.

Viscusi, W.K. (1994), 'Promoting smokers' welfare with responsible taxation', *National Tax Journal*, **XLVII** (3), 547–558.

Tokyo Round. The seventh round of multilateral negotiations by the signatories of the *General Agreement on Tariffs and Trade* (GATT). It followed the *Kennedy Round* and succeeded in reaching agreement on further tariff reductions and reductions in other barriers to trade such as import quotas. It was followed by the *Uruguay Round*.

tolerances. Revenue services normally do not consider it cost effective to assess or collect small sums which fall within certain tolerance limits. Such sums may be collected if an assessment were to be raised in any case but would not generate an assessment on their own. The level at which such tolerances are set are not normally advertised! See also *de minimis*.

toll. Originally a tax, it is now more usually used to mean the charge to cross a barrier, for example, to cross a bridge or use a road.

tourist tax. A tax on tourism which may take the form of a tax on hotel rooms or a *departure tax*.

town customs. Taxes levied in the past to maintain public works such as bridges.

trade. Trade is not defined in UK tax legislation. In *J.P. Harrison (Watford) Ltd.* v. *Griffiths* [1963] AC 1 at p. 20, Lord Denning said:

> Try as you will, the word 'trade' is one of those common English words which do not lend themselves readily to definition, but which all of us think we understand well enough. We can recognise a 'trade' when we see it, and also an 'adventure in the nature of trade'. But we are hard pressed to define it ... Short of a definition, the only thing to do is to look at the usual characteristics of a 'trade' and see how this transaction measures up to them.

Lord Wilberforce in *Ransom* v. *Higgs* [1974] 3 All ER 949 at p. 964, considered that:

> Trade involves, normally, the exchange of goods, or of services, for reward, not of all service, since some qualify as a profession, or employment, or vocation, but there must be something which the trade offers to provide by way of business. Trade, moreover, presupposes a customer ... or, as it may be expressed, trade must be bilateral – you must trade with someone!

training. See *tax training*.

training levy. A tax levied on employers to pay for the training of employees or potential employees.

transfer pricing. The use of a pricing system with respect to the transfer of goods and services within a large organisation. When used by multinational corporations, there have been suggestions that such systems have been used to transfer tax liability from higher taxed countries to lower taxed countries.

FURTHER READING
Dworin, L. (1990), 'Transfer pricing issues', *National Tax Journal*, **XLIII** (3), 285–291.
Elitzur, R. and J. Mintz (1996), 'Transfer pricing rules and corporate tax competition', *Journal of Public Economics*, **60** (3), 401–422.

transfer tax. A tax imposed in some countries on the transfer of securities.

treasury. That part of government usually entrusted with raising taxation and, sometimes, the control of public expenditure.

triangulation. This relates to trade between member states in the European Union. It is the sale of goods by a supplier in one member state to a middleman who may be resident in a second member state. The same goods are sold on to the ultimate purchaser in a third member state and the goods, as directed by the middleman, are sent directly from the supplier to the purchaser.

FURTHER READING
Doran, N. (1993), 'Triangulation', *British Tax Review*, 160–163.

tributum. A tax in ancient Rome which was levied when necessary. It was abolished in 167 BC when the spoils of war made it no longer necessary to raise large sums from Roman citizens.

tronc. A fund into which tips and service charges are paid for distribution to the staff. Such income is subject to tax. The word comes from the French for 'collecting box'.

trust. Arrangement whereby a property is held by one or more trustees for the benefit of others. See *active trust* and *bare trust*.

trustee. A person legally responsible for another person's investments or other assets.

turnover tax. A tax levied as a percentage of sales. It has been described as a cascade tax as it is levied at each stage of production when a partly finished product passes between different firms. The tax therefore includes tax paid at earlier stages of production. Such taxes are obviously higher when there are more stages of production and are likely to be economically inefficient since they provide an incentive for firms to integrate vertically. An indirect tax which avoids this effect is *value added tax* and in some countries this has replaced turnover taxes, particularly in the European Union.

Tyler, Wat (?–1381). The leader of the peasants' revolt of 1381 in which the rebels demanded the abolition of serfdom and the poll tax. One story had it that the rebellion was provoked by a tax collector insulting Wat Tyler's daughter.

U

UK tax system. The UK tax system is unusual in some ways, most notably in the way it withholds income tax at source. Its *PAYE* works on the basis of *cumulation* so that it withholds tax at source very accurately. If it works as it should most taxpayers end up with the right amount of tax withheld from their employment income and some forms of investment income. As most taxpayers are subject to the same rate of tax in the UK, the basic rate, this can be used as the appropriate rate for withholding tax on dividends and interest. The result is that the whole system operates with sufficient accuracy that most UK taxpayers are not required to complete a tax return each year.

FURTHER READING
James, S. and C. Nobes (1996), *The Economics of Taxation*, 5th edn., London: Prentice Hall.

underground economy. See *black economy*.

undistributed profits tax. A tax on company profits which have not been distributed to shareholders. See also *corporation tax*.

unearned income. See *investment income*.

unemployment trap. The situation where an unemployed person taking a job receives little or no increase in his or her *disposable income* because of the combined effects of direct taxation, the loss of welfare benefits and the need to pay additional expenses such as the costs of travel to and from work.

unfranked income. See *franked investment income*.

uniform taxes. Very *broad based taxes* levied at a single rate.

unilateral relief. Tax relief on income which has already been taxed in another country.

FURTHER READING
Oliver, J.D.B. (1993), 'Unilateral relief: The issues in *Yates v. GCA, British Tax Review*, 201–218.

unincorporated business.   An enterprise which has not been incorporated. This means that the owner(s) are subject to personal income tax but not to *corporation tax*. See *incorporation*.

unitary taxation.   A tax based on the proportion of a business's worldwide income and not just the income arising where the business is being taxed.

FURTHER READING
Sandler, D. (1994), 'Slicing the shadow – the continuing debate over unitary taxation and worldwide combined reporting', *British Tax Review*, 572–597.

unit trust.   A unit trust is a method of investment whereby 'units' are sold and the proceeds are invested in shares. It allows investors to spread their risk over all the shares the unit trust owns. The value of the units is worked out in line with the value of the unit trust's shares. The investment policy is decided by the managers but the investments are held by a separate trustee. They are also known as *mutual funds*. See also *equalisation*.

unlimited company.   A company where the members do not have *limited liability* for the debts incurred by the enterprise.

unremittable income.   Income from foreign sources which it is not possible to remit because of government action in the other country.

Uruguay Round.   The eighth round of multilateral negotiations by the signatories of the *General Agreement on Tariffs and Trade* (GATT). It followed the *Tokyo Round* and made further progress in easing tariffs and other restrictions on international trade.

user charge.   A charge to users of some services, often provided by the public sector. Some of these have features very similar to taxes but it may be thought more acceptable to call them charges.

utility.   The satisfaction or happiness that a person derives from something. It is used synonymously with economic welfare. Joan Robinson wrote that '*Utility* is a metaphysical concept of impregnable circularity' (*Economic Philosophy*, 1962, ch. 3). The concept is used in the analysis of taxation, see, for example, the *sacrifice approach.*

V

value added tax (VAT). A tax that is levied on the value added to a product at each stage of production. This means that VAT is payable at each stage of production when goods or services are supplied either to another business or to the final consumer. The tax is charged by the supplier who then passes it on to the *Customs & Excise*. The supplier is also allowed to deduct any VAT he or she has paid on inputs. For example, suppose for simplicity that the rate of VAT is 10 per cent and a firm buys some raw materials for £1000 (plus £100 VAT) and produces goods which it sells for £2000 (plus £200 VAT). The tax position would then be as follows:

	£	£
Receipts for goods	2000	
VAT charged to customer		200
Cost of raw materials	1000	
VAT charged by supplier		<u>100</u>
VAT payable to Customs & Excise		<u>100</u>

Goods and services can be treated favourably either by zero-rating or by exemption. *Zero-rated supplies* are in principle subject to VAT but the rate is zero. This means firms do not have to charge their customers VAT but can reclaim the tax paid on their inputs. Exempt goods and services are not subject to VAT, even in principle. A business cannot take any credit for the VAT paid on the supplies used to produce exempt goods. Exemption is therefore less advantageous than zero-rating, but if a good falls into both categories it is zero-rated. In the UK exempt items include:

1. Land
2. Insurance
3. Postal services
4. Betting, gaming and lotteries
5. Finance
6. Education
7. Health

8. Burial and cremation
9. Trade unions and professional bodies
10. Sports competitions
11. Certain works of art
12. Fund-raising events by charities

In the UK, VAT was introduced in 1973, replacing the previous *purchase tax* and *selective employment tax*. VAT has been levied at three rates – zero rate, a standard rate and a higher rate, but in 1979 the standard and higher rates were amalgamated into a single rate of 15 per cent. From April 1991 this was increased to 17.5 per cent.

One of the main advantages claimed for VAT has been that, by being imposed at the same rate on all goods and services, it does not distort consumers' choices. However VAT cannot, in practice, be said to have achieved this aim. Once the supplies which are zero-rated or exempt are taken into account, VAT does not cover much more than half of consumer expenditure. VAT therefore provides tax reasons for consumers to purchase some goods rather than others.

There may be policy reasons why some goods and services are given favoured tax treatment in this way. For example, it may be considered politically desirable to zero-rate food and so on, but it is not always clear that there are good reasons for such discrimination. For instance food (including caviar) is zero-rated but 'meals out' (including fish and chips) are taxable.

Another reason put forward for the introduction of VAT in the UK was harmonisation with the tax systems in the European Union. Such harmonisation is not yet complete and further changes to the coverage of the UK VAT are likely in the future. Other arguments for VAT are that it is possible to encourage exports by ensuring that all tax on them can be recovered through zero-rating. Also, VAT has been said to be 'self-policing' on the basis that if a trader does not issue an invoice then another trader is not receiving one. However invoices to final customers can be omitted and it is clear that the level of VAT evasion has been greater than anticipated by some of those who argued for its introduction. Finally the rates of VAT can be changed for macroeconomic reasons during the tax year but this provision has not been used in recent years.

FURTHER READING
Caspersen, E. and G. Metcalf (1994), 'Is a value added tax progressive? Annual versus lifetime incidence measures', *National Tax Journal*, **XLVII** (4), 731–746.

vanishing exemption. An *allowance* against income tax which is reduced as income rises until it disappears altogether.

VCT. *Venture capital trust.*

vehicle excise duty. A UK tax on motor vehicles.

Venture capital trust. Trusts which invest in unquoted companies but are quoted themselves.

vertical equity. The fairness of the tax treatment of individuals in different circumstances. For example, it might be thought fair that individuals receiving higher incomes should pay more tax than those receiving lower incomes. See also *horizontal equity.*

vice taxes. See *sin taxes.*

vocation. For the purposes of taxation, a vocation describes the way a person spends his or her life. This includes actors, authors, composers and singers.

W

Ward's Law. 'Pay nothing in tax today that you can argue about tomorrow'. Christopher Ward, *How to Complain* (1976), p. 221.

wash transaction. A sale of an asset followed shortly after by its repurchase. There may be some tax advantage in such transactions although in many tax systems there are restrictions on any such gains. See *bond washing*.

wasting asset. An asset with a limited useful life and which may be expected to decline in value.

WDA. *Writing down allowance.*

wealth. Something which has a market value and which therefore may be exchanged for money or for other assets.

wealth tax. A tax levied on net wealth. Such taxes have been a well-established part of the tax system in a number of European countries for many years. A wealth tax was introduced in The Netherlands in 1892, in Denmark in 1904, in Sweden in 1910 and in Norway in 1911. A wealth tax was also introduced in Germany in 1992, though this was based on an earlier Prussian tax of 1893. A wealth tax was introduced in Ireland in 1975 but repealed in 1978. Similarly a wealth tax was introduced in France in 1982 but abolished in 1987. In recent times the most serious proposal for introducing a wealth tax in the UK came with the Labour Government's Green Paper *Wealth Tax* in 1974. This was subsequently examined by the Select Committee on a wealth tax. The report of that committee states, somewhat briefly, that the Committee was unable to agree on a report. There then follow five minority reports, and three volumes of evidence submitted to the Committee. The five reports consist of a draft report proposed by the Chairman, a draft report proposed by the Conservative group, the Chairman's report as amended by the Committee but not adopted and two other minority reports. That was as far as the proposal got.

wear and tear.   A traditional term for *depreciation*. In the UK the relevant tax provisions are *capital allowances*.

wedges.   See *tax wedge*.

week 1 and month 1 tables.   The UK *PAYE* scheme is operated on a cumulative system. This can be suppressed by using week 1 or month 1 tables so that income tax is withheld without taking account of the amounts received and tax withheld in earlier pay periods in the tax year.

Wheatcroft, G.S.A. (1905–1987).   Distinguished tax authority and founding editor of the *British Tax Review*.

'wholly, exclusively and necessarily'.   The first part of the restrictive condition on claiming employment expenses against income taxes in the UK. To qualify the expenses must be 'wholly, exclusively and necessarily incurred in the performance of the duties of his employment'. This has been known as the 'Rule', and has been enforced very narrowly. In *Lomax v. Newton* [1953] 34 TC at pp. 561–2, Vaisey J. stated:

> I would observe that the provisions of that Rule are notoriously rigid, narrow and restricted in their operation. In order to satisfy the terms of the Rule it must be shown that the expenditure incurred was not only necessarily but wholly and exclusively incurred in the performance of the relevant official duties. And it is certainly not enough merely to assert that a particular payment satisfies the requirement of the Rule, without specifying the detailed facts upon which the finding is based. An expenditure may be "necessary" for the holder of an office without being necessary to him in the performance of the duties of that office; it may be necessary in the performance of those duties without being exclusively referable to those duties; it may perhaps be both necessary and exclusively, but still not wholly so referable. The words are indeed stringent and exacting; compliance with each and every one of them is obligatory if the benefit of the Rule is to be claimed successfully. They are, to my mind, deceptive words in the sense that when examined they are found to come to nearly nothing at all.

See also *employment expenses*.

Wicksell, Knut (1851–1926).   Swedish economist who argued, among other things, that in democracies taxation will reflect a balance among political groupings.

wilful default. A deliberate failure to what is reasonable in the circumstances.

windfall profits tax. A tax designed to extract a share of company profits gained from some unexpected good fortune.

window tax. A tax on windows, it was levied in the UK from 1651 to 1851.

withholding at source. The deduction of tax before the income is received by the taxpayer.

FURTHER READING
Soos, P.E. (1995), 'Taxation at source and withholding in England 1512 to 1640', *British Tax Review*, 49–91.

withholding tax. A tax on interest and dividends payable by a company to recipients in another country. As the domestic country cannot tax individuals in foreign countries, a withholding tax ensures the government gains at least some revenue from such payments.

World Trade Organization. Successor to the *General Agreement on Tariffs and Trade* (GATT).

FURTHER READING
Bhagwati, J. (1995), *Free Trade, 'Fairness' and the New Protectionism: Reflections on an Agenda for the World Trade Organisation*: London: Institute of Economic Affairs.

write-off. The removal from an account of an asset now considered worthless, a bad debt and so on.

writing down allowance. See *capital allowances*.

Y

year. The financial year with respect to the finance or money provided by Parliament is the 12 months to 31 March, a date established by statute in 1854. The income tax year runs to 5 April and this dates from 1832. From early times the public accounts were made up to the Michaelmas quarter day, 29 September. When the calendar was reformed in 1752 the financial year ran to 10 October. However for the financial accounts of 1800/01, the year was changed to finish on 5 January, the reformed calendar date to correspond with the old Christmas quarter day of 25 December. This was done to bring it into line with practice in commerce generally. In 1832 the Budget was presented for the year to 5 April 1833 and the supply grants were voted for the year to 31 March.

year-end adjustment. A modification of the figures after the end of a fiscal period to take account of some information not previously available. It does not normally refer to an arithmetical error.

yield. The return on an investment.

Z

zakat. A religious tax or contribution.

zero bonds. Bonds which do not pay interest but appreciate in value as they approach maturity. It is an instrument whereby 'income' may be turned into 'capital gains' and this may have tax advantages. See also *deep discount bonds*.

zero-bracket amount. US term for the income a person may receive before becoming liable to income tax.

zero-rated supplies. In a value added tax, zero rated supplies are within the system but the rate of tax applying to them is zero. This is advantageous as it means that while VAT is not charged on the consumers of the goods, businesses can reclaim the VAT paid on their inputs.

In the UK, goods and services which are zero-rated include the following:

Food, but not certain foods such as ice cream and chocolate, "meals out' and hot takeaway food and drink.
Sewerage services and water, except distilled and bottled water.
Books and so on, including newspapers and magazines.
Talking books and tape recorders for the blind and handicapped, and their repair and maintenance.
Construction of buildings and so forth. Also work done on protected buildings.
International services.
Transport. Not taxis, hire cars, and pleasure boats.
Caravans too large to be trailers and houseboats.
Gold: transactions on the London Gold Market.
Banknotes.
Drugs, medicines, medical and surgical appliances.
Clothing and footwear: clothing for young children, industrial protective clothing and motor-cyclists' crash helmets.
Export of goods.